PERGAMON INSTITUTE OF ENGLISH
(OXFORD)

Language Courses

DISCOVERING GRAMMAR

Other Titles of Interest

DISCOVERING GRAMMAR

HOWARD JACKSON

City of Birmingham Polytechnic,
England

PERGAMON INSTITUTE OF ENGLISH

a member of the Pergamon Group

Oxford · New York · Toronto · Sydney · Paris · Frankfurt

U.K.	Pergamon Press Ltd., Headington Hill Hall, Oxford OX3 0BW, England
U.S.A.	Pergamon Press Inc., Maxwell House, Fairview Park, Elmsford, New York 10523, U.S.A.
CANADA	Pergamon Press Canada Ltd., Suite 104, 150 Consumers Road, Willowdale, Ontario M2J 1P9, Canada
AUSTRALIA	Pergamon Press (Aust.) Pty. Ltd., P.O. Box 544, Potts Point, N.S.W. 2011, Australia
FRANCE	Pergamon Press SARL, 24 rue des Ecoles, 75240 Paris, Cedex 05, France
FEDERAL REPUBLIC OF GERMANY	Pergamon Press GmbH, Hammerweg 6, D-6242 Kronberg-Taunus, Federal Republic of Germany

First edition 1985

Library of Congress Cataloging in Publication Data

Jackson, Howard.
Discovering grammar.——(Language Courses)
Bibliography: p.
Includes index.
1. Grammar, Comparative and general.
I. Title.   II. Series.
P151.J26   1985   415   84–26429

British Library Cataloguing in Publication Data
Jackson, Howard.
Discovering grammar.——(Language Courses)
1. Grammar, Comparative and general
I. Title.   II. Series.
415   P151

ISBN 0–08–031517–8

Printed in Great Britain by A. Wheaton & Co. Ltd., Exeter

For

Nathan and Kirsten

Preface

The aim of this book is to provide the beginning student of linguistics with a knowledge of the scope of grammar and of the diversity of grammatical phenomena in languages. It also aims to give the reader practice in handling language data grammatically. To look at the grammatical features of some language data is to take only one of several possible perspectives on language, which together make up a complete description of a piece of language or of a whole language.

Inevitably, the English language, as the medium of this book, and as the language most familiar to the writer and possibly to the reader as well, will provide the focus of attention and the source of many examples. But it is not the intention that the grammatical description of English should in any way be regarded as normative for any other language, and much care has been exercised to include examples and data from many other languages, though these must necessarily be accompanied by English glosses.

The purpose of including 'foreign' language data is both to undermine the notion that English grammar is Grammar, and to introduce the reader to the consideration of unfamiliar language material. In this way it is hoped that the diversity of grammatical features in the languages of the world will be illustrated and at the same time the unity of the topic of grammar will be sustained.

It is intended that the book can be used both as a coursebook and self-instructionally. There are many exercises in the book, and a key is provided at the end. The symbols used in the language data either correspond to the orthography developed for the particular language or are relatable to the symbols of the International Phonetic Alphabet. A list of phonetic symbols is provided at the end.

Acknowledgments

Many of the exercises and sets of data in this book are taken, by kind permission, from *Exercises for Grammatical Analysis*, Summer Institute of Linguistics 1980. They are acknowledged in the text in the following way: "(SIL 1980: D1)", etc, to be read as: 'Exercise D1 from *Exercises for Grammatical Analysis* (SIL 1980)'.

I am grateful to Dr John Bendor-Samuel, Director of the British Summer Institute of Linguistics until 1983, and his successor, Dr Stephen Levinsohn, for their help and encouragement in the preparation of this book. I hope that they will find it worthy of the noble purpose for which SIL pursues linguistics, namely the translation of the Holy Bible.

Contents

x   Contents

1. Grammar

What is 'grammar'?

The English word *grammar* derives ultimately from the Greek *gramma*, meaning a 'letter'. In classical Greek and Latin the word *grammatica* referred to the general study of literature and language. When the word *grammar* came into English in the medieval period, it was used to refer only to Latin grammar; and it was not until the seventeenth century that the term took on a more general meaning and so had to be prefaced by 'Latin', 'English', 'French', etc.

Two meanings have competed with each other in English since the seventeenth century. In 1605 Francis Bacon wrote: "Concerning speech and words, the consideration of them hath produced the science of Grammar". While in 1637 Ben Jonson writes: "Grammar is the art of true and well speaking a Language". For Bacon, grammar is a science, a study of a set of phenomena; but for Jonson, grammar is an art, the skill or technique of speaking well. It is Jonson's definition, extended to include writing, that has predominated until recent times. Typical is the quote from an 1824 "English Grammar" by L Murray: "English grammar is the art of speaking and writing the English Language with propriety". Popularly, this is probably still what is understood by 'grammar'; but for linguists and students of language, it is Bacon's definition that is preferred.

'Grammar' vs 'a grammar'

Even having distinguished the 'science' from the 'art' definitions of 'grammar', the word is still ambiguous. On the one hand, the term 'grammar' can refer to certain features of a language, for example the "speech and words" of the Bacon quotation. That is to say that we may speak of the 'grammar of a language', being those characteristics of a language which we denote by the word 'grammar', rather than, say, the phonetic or semantic characteristics. On the other hand, the term 'grammar', or more accurately 'a grammar', is used to refer to a description either of the language as a whole (sounds, structures and meanings) or of the grammatical features of a language. A grammar in this sense is, then, a linguist's or grammarian's representation of those traits of a language designated by 'grammar' in the first sense.

Description vs prescription

Modern linguists, following Bacon's kind of definition of 'grammar', would claim to be describing the grammar of a language when they write a grammar. They would emphasise the word 'describe', in order to distinguish clearly what they are doing from the 'prescriptive' attitudes implied in the definitions of Jonson and Murray.

1

Descriptive linguists claim to be giving an account of what people actually do when they speak and write a language, rather than to be telling people what they ought to do when they speak and write their language, as the prescriptive grammarians tended to do. In the event, although different basic attitudes prevail, the distinction is probably not so clearcut as the terms 'descriptive' and 'prescriptive' imply. To be sure, prescriptive grammarians included rules in their grammars, such as "You should not end a sentence with a preposition"; but in so doing they still had to describe what a 'sentence' and a 'preposition' are. And a descriptive linguist producing a grammar of modern English, for example, has to make a choice of which English usage he is going to describe; and he would usually select the 'standard' variety, perhaps even 'standard educated usage', and by so doing he would have indulged in an implicit prescription.

'Good' and 'bad' grammar

There still remains a usage of the term 'grammar' that we have not mentioned, in instances such as: "She wrote me a nice letter, but her grammar was awful". Here the speaker is passing a judgement on someone's use of language. He is evaluating a piece of English usage against some supposed norm, called 'good English' or 'correct English'. The norm is usually what is called 'standard English' or 'educated English usage'. In other words, it is a particularly prestigious variety of English, which has achieved normative status because it is widely used in public life, and in its written form in most kinds of public communication (media, government, arts). Because it is a nationally used public variety of English does not automatically confer on it the epithet 'good', by which all alternative varieties are judged 'bad'. The use of double negation ("They didn't have none"), for example, is not intrinsically 'bad grammar'; it merely represents a 'non-standard' English usage. Linguists would prefer to replace the evaluative terms 'good' and 'bad' with the more neutral terms 'appropriate' and 'inappropriate'. That is to say, double negation may not be appropriate in the English of public communication, but in more casual or intimate circumstances among certain groups of English speakers it may well constitute a normal feature of English grammar.

Clearly, the extension of this argument is that no language can be regarded as a homogeneous entity. The term, 'the English language' subsumes a whole variety of 'Englishes', differentiated regionally and socially, one of which is the prestigious 'standard' variety, which is the variety of public communication, of the education system, and that is taught to foreign learners. When we talk of the grammar of a language, therefore, we need to specify which the variety of the language is whose grammar we are describing. Even then, we have to allow for variation within a variety; for example, in the previous sentence I used the relative pronoun *whose* to refer to the non-human noun *language*, which not all users of the 'standard' variety of English would do.

The scope of grammar

In his definition of the "science of Grammar", Bacon described the concerns of grammar as "speech and words". Certainly, words fall into the province of grammar, but it is not clear what Bacon means by 'speech'. Although the term 'grammar' was at one time used to denote the study of all aspects of a language, linguists generally restrict the scope of the term these days. The linguistic study of a language, or variety of a language, is often said to comprise three components: phonetics/phonology, grammar, semantics. The three aspects of linguistic study are, however, not independent of each other.

Phonetics and phonology are both concerned with the pronunciation of language, how language sounds, the transmission of utterances through the medium of sound. The province of phonetics is the general study of speech sounds, their articulation, acoustic qualities and range; while phonology concentrates on the use particular languages make of the available human speech sounds. Phonology deals, for example, with the number and types of distinctive speech sounds employed by a language, their arrangement in syllables and words, besides the accompanying features of stress and intonation. One point where phonology intersects with grammar is in the consideration of the way in which grammatical categories are manifested in speech sound: note, for example, the different pronunciations of the English past tense ending (-ed) in the verbs *walked, filled, loaded*.

Semantics is the study of meaning. In a way, nearly all of language study is concerned with how language means. It is arguable, indeed, that there is no study of meaning separate from the study of grammar, phonology and the like. And some linguists would replace semantics with a branch of linguistics called lexicology, which comprises the study of words, their meanings and their interrelationships. Semantics is often conceived as being wider in scope than lexicology, concerned not only with the meaning of words, but also with the meaning of sentences and with meaning relations between words and between sentences.

Language is sometimes viewed as the means by which meanings are transmitted in sound via the organising principle of grammar. Grammar is thus concerned with the counters of meaning—words, parts of words, grammatical categories—and their combination into meaningful strings—sentences, texts—prior to vocalisation through the sound system of a language. The study of grammar is often subdivided into syntax and morphology, the former dealing with the structure of sentences, and the latter with the structure of words.

Syntax

The English word *syntax* derives from a similar Greek word meaning 'arrangement' and came to refer specifically to the arrangement of words. Syntax, then, is about the ways in which words may combine with one another, with the arrangements or patterns or orders of words that are possible in a language, and with the differences in meaning that different orders of words may bring about.

Let us illustrate these points from English. The string "Every good boy deserves favours" is a possible arrangement of words in English. The following are not permissible orderings (*Note*: '*' is used to mark an ungrammatical or unacceptable string, '?' to mark a doubtful string):

*"Deserves favours every good boy"
*"Good every boy favours deserves"
*"Boy good every deserves favours"
    etc,

while "Favours deserves every good boy" could possibly be acceptable in an appropriate context, though this is perhaps doubtful. The distinction between possible and impossible, acceptable and unacceptable, is not always clearcut; native speakers of a language may vary in their judgements about the acceptability of an arrangement. (See further, Chapter 23.)

Consider now the string "Harry is tickling Susan". This is an acceptable arrangement in English, as is the following using the same words: "Susan is tickling Harry". But the two sentences do not mean the same: in the first, the person performing the action of tickling is Harry, while Susan is the one undergoing the action; in the second, their roles are reversed. Clearly, then, an alteration in the arrangement of words may bring about a change in meaning. In our investigation of syntax, therefore, we need to be able to identify elements in sentences that are movable and also determine the various functions they may perform in sentence structure.

Finally, look at the following string: "Very boy is because being atrocious naughty". This is obviously an unacceptable string in English, but it could not be made acceptable by a rearrangement of the words that it comprises. The problem lies in the incompatibility of a word like *very* with a word like *boy*, of a word like *because* with words like *is* or *being*, and of a word like *atrocious* with a word like *naughty*; although the last of these combinations could be made acceptable by converting *atrocious* into *atrociously*, giving the sequence "atrociously naughty". What these examples illustrate is that you cannot combine a word with just any other word in a language. In part, this arises from the lexical or semantic facts of a language; eg we talk about "naughty boys", but we do not usually talk about *"naughty buildings". But the incompatibilities we have been discussing do not arise particularly from the incongruities of meaning produced; rather from the grammatical, or more accurately, syntactic facts of the language. To put what we have been saying into the more precise linguistic terms we shall be using later: intensifying adverbs (like *very*) do not go together with nouns (like *boy*), conjunctions (like *because*) do not go together with verbs (like *is* and *being*), adjectives (like *atrocious*) do not go together with other adjectives (like *naughty*). Part of the task of a syntactic description is, then, to specify the possible combinations of words (more accurately, word classes—eg noun, adverb, conjunction, adjective) in a language.

Morphology

The word *morphology* derives from two Greek words which together mean 'the study of forms'. In botany, morphology is the study of plant forms. In linguistics, morphology is concerned with the grammatical structure of words; that is to say, not with the sounds or letters (or syllables) from which word forms are composed, but with constituents of words which have a grammatical function or meaning. For example, the English word *redefinitions* may be analysed into four constituents: *re-define-tion-s*. Each of these constituents occurs as a constituent in the structure of other words in the language, with the same function or meaning (eg *define*, *re-inspect-(t)ion-s*). As in syntax, so in morphology, the permissible combinations of constituents are limited: the study of morphology must, therefore, identify the possible types of word constituent in a language, investigate the patterns and arrangements of the constituents in words, and determine the function(s) or meaning(s) realised by each constituent.

The study of the morphology of a language comprises two parts. On the one hand, morphology deals with the realisation of grammatical categories, systems, or meanings (such as number—singular/plural, tense—present/past) by means of inflections. The *-s* at the end of the English examples in the previous paragraph would be considered an inflection, realising the category of plural number in English. Sometimes an inflection will realise more than one grammatical category; for example, the *-s'* of *boys'* as in "the boys' bicycles" realises both plural number and possessive case, and it is pronounced in exactly the same way as *-s* realising only plural number in *boys* and *-'s* realising only possessive case in *boy's*.

On the other hand, morphology deals with the combining of word constituents as the means of deriving new words. One of the principal ways in which a language may add new words to its vocabulary is to make neologisms from existing word constituents by making combinations that have never been made before in the language. For example, the word *redefinition* is (was) made by adding the constituent *-tion* to the constituent (in fact a potentially independent word) *define*, and the constituent *re-* to the combination *definition*; or alternatively by adding *re-* to *define*, and then *-tion* to *redefine*. It is not clear in this case which order of combination might be regarded as more plausible. Sometimes, more than two constituents may be necessary in order to make a new combination; for example, *unparalleled* in English is a combination of *un-parallel-ed*. *Unparallel* is not a possible arrangement in English, and *?paralleled* is probably at best marginal; so that we must regard *unparalleled* as a combination directly of three constituents.

Exercise 1

Say which of the following strings are grammatically unacceptable sentences of English, and explain why they are unacceptable:

1. All the birds have been migrating to warmer climates.
2. The dog big is intimidating the puppy small.
3. The baby eats not his dinner.
4. The violent wardrobe flew voraciously into the singing washing machine.
5. Every beautifully dancer receiving many into bouquet.
6. Some unhelpful decisions may not have been taken by wise men.

Exercise 2

Make as many acceptable English words as you can from the following word constituents:

1. re-
2. -ness
3. state
4. en-
5. -ment
6. large
7. -ly
8. treat

2. Word classes

Classification

From our earliest years we are taught to sort objects into groups on the basis of their similarity in one way or another. Indeed, there seems almost to be a human organisational urge to group similar things together in all kinds of areas of life. This is no less true in scientific study, where classification of phenomena forms an important part of description. In the study of language, then, we shall be grouping linguistic items into classes or types or categories on the basis of appropriate criteria of similarity.

One set of linguistic items that has traditionally been the subject of classification is that of words. In older grammars, word classes are often referred to as 'parts of speech', and the consideration of them forms the basis and main part of the grammar's content. In grammars such as these, deriving from a tradition based on Latin and Greek, eight parts of speech are recognised: Noun, Adjective, Pronoun, Verb, Adverb, Preposition, Conjunction, Interjection.

There are two problems with such a classification. One is that a classification worked out for one language may not be appropriate for another language; for instance, it is not clear where the English articles (*a*, *the*) fit into this Latin and Greek derived classification, since the classical languages did not have articles. The other problem concerns the criteria for the classification: on what basis are the words of a language grouped together into classes? One principle which emerges from this is that each language must be considered on its own terms.

Criteria of classification

One basis of classification that is applied uses semantic or 'notional' criteria, beginning from the question: What kinds of notions or concepts do the words refer to? It was this kind of criterion that gave rise to the traditional definitions of nouns as 'names of persons, places or things' and of verbs as 'doing words'. The problem with such definitions, even if they could be refined a great deal, is that they tend to remain vague and difficult to apply in any rigorous way. Such definitions are, however, useful as general characterising devices, and can serve as 'rules of thumb' in the recognition of words in an unfamiliar language.

A second basis of classification, that of morphology, is more easy to apply in a rigorous way, since it focuses on the form or structure of words; and this is not subject to the vagaries of intuitive or introspective judgements. A classification of words in English based on morphological criteria would, for example, note that one class of words (nouns) generally inflects for plural number and for possessive case (*girls*, *girl's*), while another class (verbs) inflects for past tense, present and past

6

participle (*showed*, *showing*, *shown*). Additionally, it might be noted that words containing the constituents *-tion*, *-ness*, *-ment*, *-ance* belong to the noun class (*celebration*, *keenness*, *retirement*, *remembrance*). However, derivational criteria of this kind would apply to only a small part of the membership of a class. Indeed, inflectional criteria are not necessarily universal in their application and are therefore not absolutely reliable: for example, nouns like *mud* or *information* in English do not form a plural, and the verbs *must* and *ought to* do not form a past tense or participles. Morphological criteria are not, moreover, universally applicable in the sense that some languages do not have words composed of more than one constituent, or alternatively do not have inflections regularly applying to all or most members of a class. The morphological basis of classification is, therefore, not totally reliable, though more reliable than the notional basis, and more reliably applied.

Exercise 3

In the following English data group the words into classes on the basis of their morphological characteristics:

1. big	10. fast
2. bigger	11. faster
3. biggest	12. fastest
4. read	13. grow
5. reads	14. grows
6. reader	15. grower
7. sell	16. tall
8. sells	17. taller
9. seller	18. tallest

Exercise 4

Do the same for the following Isthmus Zapotec (Mexico) data (SIL 1980: D1):

1. taburete	'chair'
2. ʃtaburetebe	'his chair'
3. ʃtaburetedu	'our chair'
4. pan	'bread'
5. ʃpanbe	'his bread'
6. ʃpandu	'our bread'
7. rukaadu	'we write'
8. rukaabe	'he writes'
9. zukaabe	'he will write'
10. bikaabe	'he wrote'
11. kukaabe	'he is writing'
12. ruʒooñedu	'we run'
13. ruʒooñebe	'he runs'
14. zuʒooñebe	'he will run'
15. biʒooñebe	'he ran'
16. kuʒooñebe	'he is running'

Syntactic criteria

A third basis for classification uses syntactic or 'functional' criteria. Words are grouped into classes according to their operation in syntactic structure: this covers both position in relation to other words and function within linguistic units. For example, we could establish a class of words in English which fitted into the frame "the _____ man", and it would include items like *good, bad, big, small, fat, thin*, etc. Generalising, we would establish the class of words that could follow a definite article (*the*) and precede a noun. It would correspond to the traditional class of adjectives, but it would be established on the basis of a clear and more-or-less absolute criterion. In English, the same set of words would also be found in the frame "'Noun' is _____" (eg "the man is good/bad/big/small, etc"). In fact, this is not entirely correct, since there is a small set of adjectives in English that can function only in the pre-noun position (eg *mere* in "a mere boy"), and a small set that functions only after verbs like *be* (eg *asleep* in "the dog is asleep"). Apart from these few exceptions, the class of adjectives in English can be defined as the set of words that functions attributively (or as a modifier) before nouns and as a complement after *be* and similar verbs.

Consider the following Portuguese data (SIL 1980: D3)

1. A   menina pequena chora pouco   'The little girl cries a little'
      the girl   little   cries a little
2. O   menino pequeno chora   'The little boy cries'
      the boy   little   cries
3. A   porca pequena come pouco   'The little sow eats a little'
      the sow   little   eats   a little
4. O   porco pequeno come muito   'The little pig eats a lot'
      the pig   little   eats   a lot
5. O   porco gordo come mais   'The fat pig eats more'
      the pig   fat   eats   more
6. A   menina gorda chora muito   'The fat girl cries a lot'
      the girl   fat   cries a lot

From this data it is possible to establish five word classes in Portuguese, on the basis of syntactic function:

1. A class of articles (*a, o*) functioning attributively before the noun.
2. A class of nouns functioning as head of the phrase functioning as subject of the sentence (*menina, menino, porca, porco*).
3. A class of adjectives functioning attributively after the noun (*pequena, pequeno, gorda, gordo*).
4. A class of verbs functioning as nucleus of the sentence (*chora, come*).
5. A class of adverbs functioning as attributive after the verb (*pouco, muito, mais*).

How many word classes?

The number of word classes that one identifies for a language will depend on the nature of the grammar of the language itself, as well as on the judgements of the linguistic analyst. Some languages are thought to have as few as three word classes. As we have already noted, a traditional 'notional' classification for English recognises eight. A more rigorous 'functional' classification might also identify eight —Noun, Verb, Adjective, Adverb, Pronoun, Determiner, Preposition, Conjunction—with various subclasses. It would seem that all languages probably have a class approximating to that of Nouns and one approximating to that of Verbs in European languages, corresponding notionally to the 'things' of experience on the one hand, and to the 'events' of experience on the other.

If we establish word classes in a language on a syntactic, functional basis, it will often be the case that we find the membership of the classes overlapping. For example, the 'words' *cut*, *bottle*, *net*, *peel*, *screw*, etc, belong to both the Noun and the Verb class in English. In such a case, where we are dealing with a small set of overlapping members, we can say either that these words have multiple class membership, or that there are two 'words' *cut*, etc, in English, one a Noun and the other a Verb. You will find that dictionaries will sometimes deal with such a word under one headword and sometimes make two headwords (eg cut[1] N, cut[2] V). If, on the other hand, two functionally established classes are completely (or almost completely) overlapping, then it is usual to talk of a single word class with multiple functions. This is the case in English with the Adjective word class, which functions both attributively before Nouns and predicatively after 'copula' verbs (eg "the tall tree"—"the tree is tall"). Only a small number of adjectives is restricted in each case to attributive or predicative position (eg "a *mere* youth", "the baby is *asleep*").

Exercise 5

Set up word classes for the following Apinaye (Brazil) data (SIL 1980: D2):

1. kukrẽ kokoi
   eats   monkey   'The monkey eats'
2. kukrẽ kra
   eats   child   'The child eats'
3. ape   kra
   works child   'The child works'
4. kukrẽ kokoi   ratʃ
   eats   monkey big   'The big monkey eats'
5. ape   kra   mɛtʃ
   works child good   'The good child works'
6. ape   mɛtʃ kra
   works well   child   'The child works well'
7. ape   ratʃ mɨ   mɛtʃ
   works a lot man good   'The good man works a lot'
8. kukrẽ ratʃ kokoi   punui
   eats   a lot monkey bad   'The bad monkey eats a lot'
9. ape   punui mɨ   piŋetʃ
   works badly man old   'The old man works badly'
10. ape   piŋetʃ   mɨ
    works a long time man   'The man works a long time'

Types of word class

It is often the case that some word classes in a language have a more readily extendable membership than others. The class membership is, in the first place, large and continually fluctuates as new words are coined and some older ones fall out of fashion or otherwise become obsolete or archaic. Such word classes in the European languages include Nouns, Verbs, Adjectives, and Adverbs. As new substances are invented or discovered, new thoughts and ideas developed, new sensations or qualities or ways of doing things and talking about things come into being, so new words are added to these word classes in the languages concerned.

These word classes are called 'open' or 'lexical' word classes: the term 'open' refers to the type of membership, while the term 'lexical' refers to the typical function of words in these classes. It is the members of these classes that carry the main burden of lexical meaning, referring to entities outside of language, in the structure of sentences. For example, note the open class words underlined in the following sentence:

"The <u>motorist</u> <u>came</u> round the <u>corner</u> and has <u>knocked</u> the <u>child</u> over".

It is predominantly the lexical words that survive in newspaper headlines and in telegrams.

The other type of word class is the 'closed' or 'grammatical' word class. Examples of these word classes in the European languages are: Pronoun, Determiner, Preposition, Conjunction. Membership of these word classes is not readily expandable and changes only slowly over time; moreover, the membership is limited and can easily be enumerated. For example, the subclass of Personal Pronouns contains the following members in modern English: *I*, *me*, *we*, *us*, *you*, *he*, *him*, *she*, *her*, *it*, *they*, *them*.

The 'grammatical' label for these word classes refers to their mainly intra-linguistic function; they constitute the cement, holding the lexical building bricks together. Determiners, like *a*, *the* or *this*, have a function within a text; similarly many pronouns, like *he* or *they*. It would be incorrect, however, to assert that members of closed classes cannot refer at all; for example, prepositions like *into*, *below* or *along* clearly refer to specific kinds of describable spatial relationships. What we have here, as so often in language, is a continuum of more-or-less rather than the discrete classifications that scientists tend to make: at the 'most lexical' end of the continuum come nouns and verbs (though not all verbs), at the 'most grammatical' (ie 'least lexical') end come determiners and some pronouns; adjectives and adverbs are more lexical than grammatical, while prepositions and conjunctions are more grammatical than lexical. Only by examining the functions of the members of each word class can this categorisation be made for a particular language.

3. Noun

Reference

Nouns refer to 'things', in the broadest sense of that term. When we choose to refer to some entity by means of a noun, we choose to view it as a 'thing'. Some entities can be referred to only by nouns: *tree*, *window*, *van*. In other instances a choice can be made. Compare the following: "The bombers destroyed the village"—"the destruction of the village by the bombers". In the first, *destroy* is a verb and the action is viewed as an 'event'; in the second, *destruction* is a noun and the action is viewed as a 'thing', about which something further may then be predicated: "The destruction of the village by the bombers was unprovoked".

The kinds of 'things' that nouns refer to are varied. If a noun refers to a 'unique' thing, it is said to be a Proper Noun, such as personal names (Wolfgang Amadeus Mozart) or names of places or institutions (Berlin, Home Office); other nouns are 'common' nouns, which refer to classes of things or to instances of things. A traditional classification of common nouns is made into 'concrete' nouns and 'abstract' nouns. 'Concrete' nouns refer to tangible, observable things, that can be defined ostensively (ie by pointing to them and saying "That is a . . ."). In some dictionaries the definition of a concrete noun includes a photograph or a line drawing; such nouns are, arguably, best defined in this way. 'Abstract' nouns, on the other hand, cannot be defined ostensively or by means of illustrations; they refer to unobservable things like *imagination* or *truth* or *feminism*. They can be defined either by giving instances or by comparing their meaning with that of other related words in the vocabulary.

A further traditional classification of nouns is into 'animate' and 'inanimate'. Animate nouns refer to living 'things', ie people, animals, birds, fish, insects, etc. Sometimes, within this group, the distinction between 'person' (ie human) and non-person is grammatically important; for example, it underlies the choice between *who* and *which* as relative pronouns in English. Inanimate nouns refer to non-living things and thus include all the abstract nouns; alternatively, one might regard the animate/inanimate distinction as being a further subclassification of concrete nouns.

Gender

We turn now from semantic classifications of nouns to grammatical ones, which have been traditionally called 'gender', since in the European languages at least such classifications are based on natural gender or sex, ie the distinction between masculine, feminine and neuter. This is not the universal basis for a grammatical classification of nouns, however. In the Algonquian languages of North America, for example, the gender classification is based on the animate/inanimate distinction. In Swahili there are six gender classes, the first containing mostly animate nouns, the second inanimate nouns, and the third plants. No gender system is completely consistent with its meaning base; there is always arbitrary assignment of words to genders from a semantic point of view, the overriding criterion has to be grammatical.

In German, for example, there are three genders: masculine, feminine and neuter. Virtually all nouns denoting male beings belong to the masculine gender, and those denoting female beings to the feminine gender, although *Weib* 'woman' and *Mädchen* 'girl' belong to the neuter gender. The neuter gender contains predominantly inanimate nouns, but these are also found in considerable numbers in the other two genders, eg *Tisch* 'table', *Baum* 'tree' are masculine, while *Blume* 'flower', *Wahrheit* 'truth' and many other abstract nouns are feminine.

There are no universal grammatical markers of gender; languages vary in the grammatical means used to signal the gender of a noun. Sometimes gender is marked in the noun itself, eg in Swahili by a set of prefixes. In French, nouns ending in *-tion* are usually feminine; in German, nouns ending in *-e* are usually feminine, as are abstract nouns in *-heit* or *-keit*. But such rules for the European languages do not account for a great number of words; here the markers of gender are outside the noun itself, usually in the forms of accompanying words like determiners or adjectives. In French, for example, the gender of a noun is identified by the form of the article accompanying it (*un*, *une* 'a'; *le*, *la* 'the' for masculine and feminine singular respectively), or by the form of a demonstrative determiner (*ce*, *cetie* 'this'/'that'), or by the form of an accompanying adjective (eg "le garçon heureux", 'the happy boy'; "la fille heureuse", 'the happy girl').

A similar picture emerges for German. The singular definite article varies in form according to the gender of the noun: *der* masculine, *die* feminine, *das* neuter. There is also variation in the adjective, especially with the indefinite article: "ein grosser Mann" 'a big man', "eine grosse Frau" 'a big woman', "ein grosses Haus" 'a big house'. The pattern of agreement is, in fact, more complex than this, as there is a tendency to mark gender once only in any noun phrase.

Some languages do not make a gender classification of their nouns, for example Quechuan languages. It is arguable, moreover, that English does not exhibit grammatical gender: there is no mark of gender in the noun, apart from one or two endings that are restricted to nouns referring to females (eg *tigress*, *usherette*); and there is no mark in accompanying words (articles, adjectives, etc) either. The only argument for gender in English would be on the basis of the substitutability by a third person singular pronoun (ie *he*, *she* or *it*): this usage corresponds almost exactly with natural gender, except that *she* is sometimes extended in usage to refer to ships, cars, mountains, and there is variability of usage when referring to animals.

Exercise 6

Arrange the nouns in the following Chontal of Tabasco (Mexico) data (SIL 1980: C7) into genders, indicating how each gender is marked:

1. unkʔe hun	'one paper'		13. untu winik	'one man'
2. uʃkʔe hun	'three papers'		14. uʃtu winik	'three men'
3. wəkʔe hun	'six papers'		15. wʔtu winik	'six men'
4. untu tsitam	'one pig'		16. unkʔe wah	'one tortilla'
5. uʃtu tsitam	'three pigs'		17. uʃkʔe wah	'three tortillas'
6. wətu tsitam	'six pigs'		18. wəkʔe wah	'six tortillas'
7. untsʔit əhin	'one alligator'		19. untu mut	'one bird'
8. uʃtsʔit əhin	'three alligators'		20. uʃtu mut	'three birds'
9. wətsʔit əhin	'six alligators'		21. wətu mut	'six birds'
10. unkʔe jopo	'one leaf'		22. untsʔit tsan	'one snake'
11. uʃkʔe jopo	'three leaves'		23. uʃtsʔit tsan	'three snakes'
12. wəkʔe jopo	'six leaves'		24. wətsʔit tsan	'six snakes'

Countability

Many nouns refer to objects that are countable. The noun may be preceded or followed by a numeral indicating how many of the objects are being referred to, eg *six boxes*. Very often, the fact that more than one is being referred to is also marked in the noun (*boxes* rather than *box*). Besides numerals, quantity may also be indicated by 'indefinite' quantifiers, which do not specify an exact number, eg *several boxes*, *a lot of boxes*, *a few boxes*. Nouns, whose quantity may be specified in these ways, are called 'countable' nouns.

Some nouns refer to things that may not be counted. For example, it is not possible in English to speak of **six waters*. A plural form of the noun does not occur, and the quantifier *some* occurs before the singular form of the noun to indicate indefinite quantity: *some water* (compare *some boxes*—plural, but not **some box*). Such nouns are called 'uncountable' or 'mass' nouns. With some mass nouns in English a numeral may occur, but the meaning is not 'plural' but 'kinds of', eg *six wines*, *six cheeses*.

Number

Number is a grammatical category applicable to nouns when they are countable. Such nouns are often marked in languages for 'plural' number. That is to say, we may distinguish 'singular' number (referring to one) from 'plural' number (referring to more than one). Singular nouns do not usually have a positive mark for number: they are said to be 'unmarked'; it is plural number that is usually marked in nouns. Not all languages mark their nouns for number, and some only mark number when the noun is not accompanied by any other indication of quantity in the form of a numeral, indefinite quantifier, etc. Some languages, in addition to plural number, also mark a separate 'dual' number, when a noun refers to two objects.

Number is usually marked in nouns by means of suffixes (endings) or prefixes (added to the front). In European languages suffixation is the most common method. For example, in English, the regular mark of a plural is the (written) suffix -(*e*)*s*, eg *apples*, *apricots*, *peaches*. It might be noted that the pronunciation of the plural suffix is different for each of these three words, a point that will be taken up in Chapter 8. It might also be noted that, although suffixation by -(*e*)*s* is the regular way of marking plural number in nouns in English, it is also marked in several other ways: compare, for example, *man—men*, *mouse—mice*, *ox—oxen*.

In German there are five different kinds of suffix to mark plural, three of which may in addition be accompanied by a change in the vowel of the noun (called 'umlaut', indicated in writing by '¨' above the vowel concerned). The first suffix is *-e*, with a noun like *Monat—Monate* 'months', and with umlaut in *Sohn—Söhne* 'sons'. The second suffix is *-(e)n*, with a noun like *Schmerz—Schmerzen* 'pains' or *Biene—Bienen* 'bees'; this suffix does not occur with umlaut. The third suffix is a 'zero'; that is, there is no ending, the plural is the same as the singular, as in a noun like *Daumen—Daumen* 'thumbs', or just with umlaut as in *Mantel—Mäntel* 'coats'. The fourth suffix is *-er*, with a noun like *Bild—Bilder* 'pictures', and with umlaut in *Rad—Räder* 'wheels'. The fifth and least frequent plural suffix, which is restricted mainly to words borrowed from other languages, especially English and French, is *-s*, as in a noun like *Park—Parks*; it does not occur with umlaut.

Number and gender

In some languages the marking of number and gender intersects. This is true to a limited extent for German: the *-e* suffix tends to be associated with masculine nouns, the *-(e)n* suffix with feminine nouns, and the *-er* suffix with neuter nouns. In Latin the intersection is more systematic: for example, *corvus—corvi* 'crow/s' represents a masculine plural, while *puella—puellae* 'girl/s' represents a feminine plural, and *bellum—bella* 'war/s' a neuter plural.

Consider the following data (SIL 1980: C8) from Konkomba (Ghana):

1. libil libaa	'one year'		7. kidʒuk kibaa	'one knife'
2. bubib bugmu	'five years'		8. ndʒum mulee	'two knives'
3. lilal libaa	'one axe'		9. kipipeek kibaa	'one place'
4. bulab bulee	'two axes'		10. npipeem mugmu	'five places'
5. lidʒool libaa	'one hill'		11. kigbalik kibaa	'one spear'
6. budʒoob buniin	'eight hills'		12. ngbalim muniin	'eight spears'

The nouns in this data are: *-bi-* 'year', *-la-* 'axe', *-dʒoo-* 'hill', *-dʒu-* 'knife', *-pipee-* 'place', *-gbali-* 'spear'. The first three of these (in Nos 1–6) belong to one gender, as marked by one set of prefixes and suffixes; the remaining three belong to a second gender, being marked by another set of prefixes and suffixes. The numeral (*-baa* 'one', *-lee* 'two', *-gmu* 'five', *-niin* 'eight') is also marked (by prefixes) according to the gender of the noun. The gender markers are, however, different in singular and plural. The markers of number thus intersect with the markers of gender, so that any prefix/suffix marks at the same time both a number (singular or plural) and a gender (1 or 2), according to the following scheme:

			Noun		Numeral
Gender 1	⎱	sing	li-	-l	li-
eg *-bi-* 'year'	⎰	pl	bu-	-b	bu-
Gender 2	⎱	sing	ki-	-k	ki-
eg *-dʒu-* 'knife'	⎰	pl	n-	-m	mu-

Case

Case is a further grammatical category that is marked in the noun and additionally (or alternatively) in words that accompany nouns (eg articles, adjectives). The function of case is to signal the grammatical/semantic relationships between nouns in a larger syntactic structure (eg clause or sentence). Languages vary in the extent to which case marking is used to signal these relationships. For example, in German the article (not the noun) is sometimes marked to signal whether the noun is functioning as Subject or Object in a sentence (see Chapter 11 for discussion of 'Subject', 'Object' and similar terms). In the following German sentence: "Der Hund hat den Mann gebissen"—'The dog bit the man', the noun *Hund* 'dog' is marked as Subject of the sentence by the form of the definite article *der* 'the', while *Mann* 'man' is marked as Object by the form of the definite article *den*. In English, on the other hand, the grammatical relationships 'Subject-of' and 'Object-of' are signalled merely by the relative ordering of the elements in the sentence. So, "The man bit the dog" has a different Subject and Object from "The dog bit the man"; while "Den Mann hat der Hund gebissen" has the same Subject and Object as "Der Hund hat den Mann gebissen".

There is a great variation in the number and kinds of case marking found in different languages. Some languages (eg Chinese) do not mark case at all. In English case marking in the noun is limited to a 'possessive' (or 'genitive') case, marked in writing by -*'s* in the singular noun and by -*s'* in the plural noun; it links two nouns in a semantic relationship of 'belonging' or 'possession' (eg "the cow's tail", "the girl's name") or in some kind of largely grammatical relationship (eg "the world's end", "the enquiry's conclusions"). In the pronoun in English, however, some distinctions are made between subject and object forms, eg *I—me*, *she—her*, *they—them*.

Four cases are distinguished in German, marked most consistently in the article: nominative, accusative, dative, genitive. The nominative and accusative are the Subject and Object cases respectively, mentioned earlier. The dative marks the Indirect Object in a sentence, eg *seiner Frau* '(to) his wife' in the following sentence: "Der Mann hat seiner Frau einen Brief geschickt", 'The man sent his wife a letter'. The genitive in German functions like the genitive/possessive in English. In addition, all the cases except the nominative are governed (see Chapter 16) by particular prepositions, eg *für* 'for' is followed by noun phrases in the accusative case, *von* 'by'/'from' by those in the dative, and *während* 'during' by those in the genitive. Latin has a further case, additional to the four found in German: the ablative, which usually translates into English by means of the prepositions *by*, *with* or *from*.

In Punjabi a 'direct' and an 'oblique' case are distinguished. The oblique case is used before postpositions (in common with other North-Indian languages, Punjabi has postpositions, coming after the noun referred to, rather than prepositions). The direct case is used for subjects and objects, although under certain circumstances these are realised by a noun in the oblique case followed by a particular postposition. In addition to the direct and oblique, Punjabi marks a 'vocative' case on nouns used as forms of address, an 'instrumental' case (in the plural only) to signal the object 'with' which an action is performed, an 'ablative' case to signal movement 'from' a place, and a 'locative' case to signal 'at' a place.

In some languages, known as 'ergative' languages, the case of the Object of a transitive verb (for explanation of this term, see Chapter 10) is the same as that of the Subject of an intransitive verb. Such a language is Alawa, spoken in Australia. Among other cases, Alawa has a 'nominative', which is unmarked, and an 'operative', which is marked by a suffix. The nominative is used for the Subject of intransitive verbs and the Objects of transitive verbs; while the operative is used for the Subject of transitive verbs, as well as the instrument or location involved in an action. Consider the following examples:

```
lilmi        na-wutala gutaru            'The man came to a hill'
man (nom) he-went  hill (nom)
lilmi-ri    yaŋ ka-ŋatan-na da kiribu        parakal-ta
man (op) hit  he-did-it      kangaroo (nom) spear (op)
                                  'The man killed the kangaroo with a spear'
```

Exercise 7

For the following Basari (Ghana) data (SIL 1980: C2), identify what the genders are and how they are marked for singular and plural in the noun and the demonstrative:

1. uni umbini	'this person'	biniib bimbini	'these persons'
2. ubɔti umbini	'this chief'	bibɔtiib bimbini	'these chiefs'
3. diyin dimbini	'this name'	ayin ŋimbini	'these names'
4. dibil dimbini	'this seed'	abil ŋimbini	'these seeds'
5. kusaau kumbini	'this farm'	tisaati timbini	'these farms'
6. kukabuu kumbini	'this basket'	tikabuti timbini	'these baskets'

4. Verb

Reference

Verbs refer to 'events'. Included under the heading of 'event' are: actions, eg *spill* in "The cat has spilled the milk"; 'process', eg *spill* in "The milk has spilled"; 'happenings', eg *occur* in "The accident occurred at lunch-time". One may also need to extend the notion of 'event' to include 'states', expressed in English by verbs like *seem*, *look* ("She seems/looks tired"), and above all *be* ("She is happy"). In the case of *be* in particular, however, two points might be noted. Firstly, many languages would not have the 'copula' verb *be* in sentences like "She is happy"; ie it would be equivalently "She happy" (cf Punjabi "ik pətla" = 'One (is) thin'). Secondly, it has been argued that for languages like English one should regard the 'verb' in sentences like "She is happy" as 'be happy'. The effect of this suggestion would be to vastly increase the number of verbs in a language like English, by including the majority of adjectives, and possibly many nouns as well (cf "She is a doctor"). One may well decide that the implementation of such a suggestion would not result in a very economical description of the language, since one would still need, for example, to account for the attributive use of adjectives in English (eg "the happy girl").

From the examples above ("The cat has spilled the milk"—"The milk has spilled") we can see that there may exist a relationship between actions and processes. Indeed, the use of *spill* in the first of these examples is sometimes referred to as an 'action-process', to distinguish it from action verbs that do not imply a simultaneous process, such as *laugh* in "Everybody laughed", or *kick* in "The referee has kicked the ball into the goal". Processes do not necessarily presuppose some action in order to trigger them off; all that is implied is some change taking place in the 'thing' undergoing the process, eg "The sky has cleared", "The leaves are turning yellow".

Tense

One piece of information that languages often encode with relation to events is the time when they take place, specifically either before the time of speaking, at the time of speaking, or after the time of speaking. These real-world time differences are encoded in language by means of the grammatical category of 'tense'. We thus often find verbs marked for 'past', 'present' and 'future' tenses, for example in French: "il parlait" 'he talked', "il parle" 'he talks', "il parlera" 'he will talk'.

In French, then, tense is marked by suffixes in the verb. Not all languages mark tense in this way; the English translations given for the French examples show that English marks present and past tense by means of suffixes (-*s* for present, and -*ed*

17

for past), but the future tense is marked periphrastically, by using another, 'auxiliary', verb. In fact, it is disputable whether a future tense can be clearly recognised in English, since it is possible to refer to future time in a number of ways, eg "he is going to talk", "he is to talk". Some languages do not mark tense in the verb by means of prefixes or suffixes at all, but by the use of auxiliary verbs or particles (see Chapter 9). In the Yurok language (North America), for example, tense is indicated by a series of particles placed before the verb, eg "ho sʔegok" = 'past they-box', ie "they boxed". Other languages do not mark tense at all, but instead have an elaborate system of 'aspects' (see below); this seems to be the case in Classical Arabic.

We have suggested so far that tense, encoding real-world time, distinguishes past, present and future. These are not, however, the only time relations that may be encoded in language; they are time-relations viewed from the perspective of the time of speaking, the present. Some languages encode time relations that might be referred to as 'past-in-the-past' and 'past-in-the-future', eg in English "He had finished his breakfast, when . . .", "He will have completed the report by Thursday". The first of these sets one event in a past previous to another past event, while the second views an event as being past from a future perspective. These tenses are sometimes referred to as 'pluperfect' and 'future perfect' respectively.

Additionally, in some languages we find that there is no single past tense form, for example. Such is the case in French, where there are three past tenses, called the 'imperfect', 'preterite' and 'perfect'. A distinction between preterite and perfect is maintained in written French: the perfect implies that a past event has relationship to the present (eg "Jean m'a écrit deux fois cette semaine"—'John has written to me twice this week'), while the preterite places an event unequivocally in the past (eg "Jean lui écrivit à Noël"—'John wrote to him at Christmas'). In spoken French, however, the perfect has taken over the functions of the preterite, so that the latter is now restricted to the written form of the language. The imperfect should perhaps be considered under aspect (see below) rather than tense: it indicates 'past with duration' (eg "Il écrivait au moment où le téléphone sonna"—'He was writing when the telephone rang'), or 'past event repeated' (eg "Je lui écrivais chaque jour"—'I wrote to him every day'). But the imperfect in French is also used for past description ("Elle avait les cheuveux blonds"—'She had blond hair') and may be interchangeable with the preterite or perfect (eg "Il décidait soudain de se lever"—'He suddenly decided to get up").

Tense and time

Our discussion of tense up to now has centred on its relationship with time. But tense, although it clearly relates to real-world time, is nevertheless independent of it, in the sense that on occasions tense distinctions may have nothing to do with time. This independence of tense and time may be illustrated by the fact that they may not be in a one-to-one relationship in a language. Consider the 'present' tense in English: it may refer to present time, eg "I see no ships". But it may also be timeless in its reference, eg "The sun rises in the east", "Oil floats on water". It may be used with future reference, eg "Father comes home tomorrow"; or with reference to habitual events, eg "We go shopping on Fridays". And in a few instances in English a present tense verb may refer to a past event, eg "I hear that you've changed your job", when the hearing was presumably before the time of speaking. A further illustration of this lack of one-to-one correspondence between tense and time is the perfect tense in German: on the one hand it is used like the perfect in French; on the other it may have a future-perfect reference, eg "Bald hat er es geschafft"—'He will have soon done it'.

The independence of tense and time is also evident in the fact that tenses may be used for other than time reference. The only difference in English between "May I use your telephone?" (present) and "Might I use your telephone?" (past) is one of tentativeness or politeness: the *might*-form is interpreted as a more polite request than the *may*-form. Similarly in conditional clauses in English, present tense implies a 'real' condition while past tense implies a 'hypothetical' condition, and both refer to future time: compare "If you visit the museum tomorrow . . .", "If you visited the museum tomorrow . . .". One might also point to the use of the present tense in past narratives (the so-called 'historic present') in order to mark a particular episode as climactic or to bring it into particular focus for some reason; spoken narratives in some styles of speaking are entirely in the present tense.

Tense and person

While dealing with tense we need to note that the marking of tense in the verb by means of suffixes (or prefixes) sometimes intersects with the marking of person/number. The category of person is dealt with in detail in the next chapter; let us note for the moment the distinction between the speaker (1st person singular/plural—*I/we*), the addressee (2nd person singular/plural—*you* for both in English), and the thing/person talked about (3rd person singular/plural—*he, she, it/they*). In the past tense in English, there is no mark of person along with that of tense: *-ed* signals past tense for all persons/numbers ("I talked", "you talked", "he talked", "we talked", "they talked"). In the present tense, there is a mark for the 3rd person singular, but for none of the other person/numbers ("he talks" but "I talk", "you talk", etc).

In French, on the other hand, each tense is marked by a different set of person-/number suffixes, so that each suffix is at the same time a mark of tense and person-/number, with very little overlap between forms. Consider the following table of forms for the verb *parler* 'speak', 'talk':

	Imperfect	Present	Future
1st sing *je*	parlais	parle	parlerai
2nd sing *tu*	parlais	parles	parleras
3rd sing *il/elle*	parlait	parle	parlera
1st pl *nous*	parlions	parlons	parlerons
2nd pl *vous*	parliez	parlez	parlerez
3rd pl *ils/elles*	parlaient	parlent	parleront

The relative absence of overlap between forms applies primarily to the written form of the language; there is far more overlap in the spoken language, eg the 1st, 2nd and 3rd person singular and the 3rd person plural forms of the imperfect are identical in pronunciation, as are the same forms of the present. Spoken French has diverged quite radically from the written form, which represents an older pronunciation.

Consider now the following data (SIL 1980: A3) from Mbembe (Eastern Nigeria):

1. nwa ogwo   'the child drinks'
2. nwa oci   'the child eats'
3. nwa oci eten   'the child eats fish'
4. aci eten   'you eat fish'
5. oci eten   'he eats fish'
6. nwa mogwo   'the child will drink'
7. maci eten   'you will eat fish'
8. kogwo   'he does not drink'
9. kagwo   'you do not drink'.

By comparing Nos 1 and 2 we can conclude that *nwa* means 'child', and *ogwo* and *oci* 'drinks' and 'eats' respectively. No 3 adds the further vocabulary item *eten* 'fish'. Nos 4 and 5 show us that the person is marked in the verb by means of a prefix, *o-* for 3rd person singular, *a-* for 2nd person: the verbs 'drink' and 'eat' are in fact then *-gwo*, *-ci*. Nos 6 and 7 show us that future tense is also marked in the verb with a prefix, independently of person and prior to it in order: *m-*. We conclude that present tense is *un*marked. Nos 8 and 9 show us additionally that the negative is marked in the verb by means of a prefix (*k-*), independently of person, though our data does not allow us to draw conclusions about its relationship to tense.

Exercise 8

Identify the constituents of the verbs in the following Congo Swahili data (SIL 1980: A2), and list them with their meanings:

1. ninasem   'I speak'
2. wunasem   'you speak'
3. anasem   'he speaks'
4. wanasem   'they speak'
5. ninaon   'I see'
6. nilion   'I saw'
7. ninawaon   'I see them'
8. niliwuon   'I saw you'
9. ananion   'he sees me'
10. wutakanion   'you will see me'

Now translate 'they saw him' into Congo Swahili.

Aspect

In addition to encoding in the verb the time at which an event takes place, many languages encode various ways of viewing the event, particularly from the point of view of the extension of the event in time. Ways of viewing the event are encoded in language by means of the grammatical category of 'aspect'. One aspect that is frequently found is the one we have already noted in the French imperfect: the 'durative', also termed 'continuous' and 'progressive'. The durative encodes a view of the event that regards it as having duration, continuing through a period of time, or being in progress. The English 'progressive' is an aspect with a similar meaning: compare "He slept all day" with "He was sleeping all day". The first views the sleeping as a once-and-for-all past event, the second views it as an event that has duration: the event is the same, the way of viewing it differs.

Another aspect that is often marked in languages is the 'completive' or 'perfective', which views an event as completed or finished rather than not yet completed. The difference in meaning may be illustrated from English with the following examples: "I was reading a book last night"—"I read a book last night". The first, in the past progressive form, implies an uncompleted event, while the second, in the simple past form, implies a completed event—the book was finished. A perfective aspect is found commonly in Slavonic languages among others. For example, in Polish one finds a set of perfective verbs contrastive with an equivalent set of imperfective verbs, eg *mrugnąć* (perfective) 'to blink once'—*mrugać* (imperfective) 'to blink several times', *zaboleć* (perfective) 'to begin aching'—*boleć* (imperfective) 'to ache', *domówić* (perfective) 'to finish speaking'—*mówić* (imperfective) 'to speak'.

As a counterpart to the continuous aspect, some languages positively mark a 'punctiliar' aspect: the event is viewed as taking place at a point in time. This is done in Alawa (Australia); compare the following forms: *ŋawiña* 'I will go' (future, no aspect marking), *ŋadiña* 'I can go' (present, punctiliar), *ŋadiři* 'I can go' (present, continuous).

As with tense, aspect may be marked in the verb by means of affixes (as in Alawa); or periphrastically with auxiliary verbs, as in the English progressive, which is formed with *be* as an auxiliary followed by a present participle (*is going*, *was talking*); or by means of particles.

Consider the following Ekpeye (Eastern Nigeria) data (SIL 1980: A6); there is no marker for 'future':

1.	edi	'he will eat'
2.	edikpo	'he will finish eating'
3.	edilɛ	'he has eaten'
4.	adikpolɛ	'we have finished eating'
5.	edikpohwɔ	'he will eventually finish eating'
6.	adigbalɛ	'we have eaten again'
7.	edikpohwɔlɛ	'he has eventually finished eating'
8.	emegba	'he will make again'
9.	amekpogbalɛ	'we have finished making again'
10.	amegbahwɔ	'we will eventually make again'

From the English glosses it is clear that a number of aspects are marked in the verb in Ekpeye, translated by English 'have', 'finish', 'eventually', 'again'. They are marked by the suffixes *-lɛ*, *-kpo*, *-hwɔ*, *-gba* respectively; and they occur in the order *-kpo-gba-hwɔ-lɛ*. The aspects might be termed 'perfect' (*-lɛ*), 'completive' (*-kpo*), 'culminative' (*-hwɔ*), 'iterative' (*-gba*). To complete the analysis, *-di-* 'eat' and *-me-* 'make' are the verbs, while *e-* 'he' and *a-* 'we' are person prefixes.

Exercise 9

Identify the constituents of the verb words in the following Inga (Colombia) data (SIL 1980: A7), and suggest terms for the aspects that are marked (*Note*: 3rd person singular is unmarked):

1. chayarca   'he arrived'
2. chayacurca   'he was arriving'
3. chayarcani   'I arrived'
4. chayacurcanimi   'I was definitely arriving'
5. chayacumi   'he is definitely arriving'
6. chayamucunimi   'I am definitely arriving here'
7. chayamurcachar   'he probably arrived here'
8. chayamucurcanguichar   'you were probably arriving here'
9. puñucuchar   'he is probably sleeping'

5. Pronoun

Types of pronoun

The term 'pronoun' implies an item which stands for or instead of a noun. In general, pronouns can be used in grammar where nouns would normally function, as Subject of a sentence, Object of a sentence, and so on. The class of pronouns, however, is not homogeneous; there are several types of pronoun.

Perhaps the words most commonly thought of as pronouns are those represented by the English set *I/me, you, he/him, she/her, it, we/us, they/them*. These are the 'personal' pronouns. It is to be expected that a similar set of pronouns would be more or less universal, although not necessarily with all the distinctions found in the English set.

Allied to the personal pronouns one may also find a set of 'reflexive' pronouns, eg in English *myself, yourself, himself, herself, itself, ourselves, yourselves, themselves*. In English these have two uses: when the Object of a sentence is the same as the Subject (eg "she has hurt herself"); and as an emphatic pronoun (eg "I did it myself"). Many languages do not have such an elaborate system of reflexive or emphatic pronouns; one form may well serve for all persons, as in North-Indian languages. In German the reflexive pronoun is the same as the accusative case form of the personal pronoun for 1st and 2nd persons, with a special form for 3rd person (singular and plural) – *sich*, eg "Ich habe mich verletzt" 'I have hurt myself', "Sie hat sich verlatzt" 'she has hurt herself'. The emphatic pronoun in German is an invariant form—*selbst*, eg "Ich habe es selbst gemacht" 'I did it myself'.

Also related to the personal pronouns one may find a set of 'possessive' pronouns, eg in English *mine, yours, his, hers, its, ours, theirs*, used in sentences like "This coat is yours" (ie '... belongs to you'), or "Mine is the brown one" (ie '(the coat) belonging to me ...').

Other types of pronoun found in languages include: 'relative' pronouns, used to introduce relative clauses (see Chapter 13), eg *who, which, whose, that* in English; 'interrogative' pronouns, used in questions, eg *who?, what?* in English; 'indefinite' pronouns, used to refer to a non-specified person or thing, eg *someone, anything, everybody* in English; 'demonstrative' pronouns, with a distinguishing or pointing reference, *this/these, that/those* in English, eg in "That is a good idea", "This looks like the one we want".

Person

We noted in the previous chapter that probably all languages have a grammatical category of person, distinguishing a 1st, 2nd and 3rd person, referring to the speaker, the addressee, and the person/thing being talked about, respectively.

Unless, unusually, the reference of a 3rd person pronoun is clear in the situational context, a 3rd person pronoun will have a textual function: it will be standing for a noun occurring previously in the text; eg "Once upon a time there was an *emperor*. *He* ruled the country harshly". The reference of 1st and 2nd person pronouns is clear in the situational context, ie the person talking and the person being talked to, respectively.

Many languages have more than one 2nd person pronoun; indeed, English appears to be unusual in having only one. In French, for example, we find *tu* and *vous*. Although *vous* is the plural counterpart to singular *tu*, it is also used to speak to a singular addressee. A distinction is made in terms of familiarity or politeness: *tu* is used when talking to family or friends, *vous* with strangers. But the distinction is also connected with relative social status: a social superior may speak to a social inferior (eg adult to child, master to servant) with *tu*, expecting to be addressed with *vous* in return. This use of 2nd person pronouns to signal social asymmetry has, however, been gradually breaking down in the increasing egalitarianism of post-war society. Similarly in German: *du*, which has its own plural form *Ihr*, is the 'familiar' 2nd person pronoun, and *Sie* the 'polite' one, used for both singular and plural. A further level of politeness or deference may be added by using a 3rd person form of address; this may also be found in English, in deferential butler-talk, eg "My lord has requested the car. Would he like a rug?"

In Javanese there are three 2nd person pronouns, whose use depends on whether one is addressing a superior, an equal, or an inferior in social status; although how many of these an individual may use will depend on his own social status, and in Javanese it is not only 2nd person pronouns that are marked for social status but other vocabulary items as well (eg there are three forms for 'now', two for 'rice', etc). Similarly, in Hindi and Urdu there are three 2nd person pronouns, one for addressing inferiors, one for addressing intimates, and one for expressing politeness or respect. In Bengali there are also 'ordinary' and 'honorific' forms of the 3rd person pronoun.

Person and number/gender/case

We have already mentioned that number intersects with person in the pronoun system; that is to say, pronouns occur in singular and plural forms for each person. In the case of 2nd and 3rd person pronouns the reference is to a plurality of addressees or things under discussion, eg *Ihr*, *they*. But with 1st person pronouns we do not have a straightforward case of plurality; unless the speaker is a chorus, 1st person plural must refer to 1st person (*I*) plus others. Now 'others' could include either the addressee (*you*) or persons other than the addressee (*they*) or both together. Some languages encode these possible distinctions by having more than one 1st person plural pronoun: an 'exclusive' 1st person plural pronoun (ie *I* + *they*, but not *you*), and an 'inclusive' 1st person plural pronoun (ie *I* + *you*, and also possibly *they*). Alternatively, a distinction may be made, as in Alawa (see below), between *I* + *you* but not *they*, and *I* + *you/they*.

Usually only in the 3rd person, person also intersects with gender, often reflecting the gender distinctions made in the noun class. In French, for example, a masculine/feminine distinction is made in both singular and plural 3rd person pronouns: *il/elle*, *ils/elles*. In German the masculine/feminine/neuter gender distinction is found only in the 3rd person singular pronoun (*er, sie, es*), the plural pronoun being common for all genders (*sie*). A similar pattern is found in English, where the 3rd person singular pronoun is the only place in the language that a gender distinction is maintained (*he, she, it*). In Punjabi we find the reverse case: the masculine/feminine gender distinction of nouns is not replicated in the 3rd person pronoun.

A third intersection of grammatical categories may occur in the pronoun between person and case, affecting potentially all person/numbers. English makes a case distinction (subject/object) in the personal pronoun system, though no longer anywhere else in the language, eg *I/me*, *she/her*. In fact, the 'subject'/'object' labels represent a simplification: the *I*-forms are restricted to subject position, though native speakers argue about whether one says "It is I" or "It's me" (cf the less likely "It's I", "It is me"); but the *me*-forms are used everywhere else in the structure of sentences, as object ("They saw me"), after a preposition ("Don't wait for me"), as an emphatic ("Who's coming?"—"Me!").

Pronoun systems

We will now diagram two personal pronoun systems, to show how the categories we have been discussing intersect to produce an array of pronoun forms.

German:

		Nominative	Accusative	Dative
sing	1	ich	mich	mir
	2 familiar	du	dich	dir
	3 m	er	ihn	ihm
	3 f	sie	sie	ihr
	3 n	es	es	ihm
pl	1	wir	uns	uns
	2 familiar	ihr	euch	euch
	2 sing/pl polite	Sie	Sie	Ihnen
	3	sie	sie	ihnen

It will be noted that the 2nd person 'polite' forms are identical in pronunciation with the 3rd person plural, although situational context will always disambiguate them. In writing, it is conventional to capitalize the initial letter of the 2nd person forms.

Alawa (Australia):

	Direct	Indirect
sing 12	ñanu	ñaka
1	ŋina	ŋapa
2	ñagana	ñaba
3 m	nula	nipa
3 f	ŋadula	ŋatu
non-sing 12	ñalu	ñalaŋa

Alawa (Australia) (cont.)

	Direct	Indirect
dual 1	ŋařu	ŋařaŋa
2	wuřu	wuřuŋa
3	yiřula	yiřuŋa
pl 1	ŋalu	ŋalaŋa
2	wulu	wuluŋa
3	yilula	yiluŋa

In Alawa a case distinction is made between 'direct' and 'indirect': the direct pronoun is used for the Subject of most clauses and wherever a pronoun is placed at the beginning of a clause for emphasis; the indirect pronoun is used elsewhere in the clause and for possession. The usual three persons are distinguished, together with an additional 1st person, marked '12': in the singular, this person refers to the speaker plus one hearer, in the non-singular to the speaker plus two or more hearers. Three numbers are distinguished for 1st, 2nd and 3rd persons singular, dual and plural. In the 3rd person singular a gender distinction (masculine/feminine) operates. There are no overlaps among the twenty-four forms of the personal pronoun.

Bound and free pronouns

The pronouns that we have discussed so far in this chapter all have the status of free and independent words. In the previous chapter we noted that person/number is also frequently marked in the verb by means of a prefix or suffix, eg in French or Congo Swahili. However, these two languages differ in the way in which they mark person in the verb: in the case of French the category of person intersects with that of tense, so that a particular suffix signals both person and tense simultaneously, eg "je parle", "je parlais", "je parlerai"—where -e, -ais and -erai mark both 1st person and present, imperfect and future tenses respectively. In the case of Swahili (Exercise 8) the category of person is marked independently of the category of tense: ni-, wu-, a-, and wa- are person prefixes, while na-, li- and taka- are tense prefixes. When person is marked in this way in the verb, independently of tense and aspect in particular (as categories that do not intersect with person in free pronouns), then we are justified in talking about a set of bound pronoun forms. Many languages exhibit parallel sets of free and bound pronouns.

Consider the system of personal pronouns in Bimoba (Ghana):

	Emphatic free	Non-emphatic free	Bound subject	Bound object
sing 1	min	n	m-/ma-	-n
2	fin	a	f-/fa-	-a
3 animate	ngɔɔ	u	w-/wu-	-u/-ɔ
pl 1	timm	te	t-	-et
2	yimm	i	y-/yi·	-i
3 animate	ngamm	be	b-	-eb
sing/pl 3 inanimate	ngann	le	l-	-er

Bimoba has two sets of free pronouns, one used in emphatic contexts, the other when the pronoun is not being emphasised. There are also two sets of bound pronouns, distinguished for case: a subject set, and an object set. The pronouns are distinguished for the usual three persons, and for singular and plural number. In the 3rd person a gender distinction is made between 'animate' and 'inanimate', and the 3rd person inanimate pronoun shows no distinction of number.

Exercise 10

In the following Zulu data (SIL 1980: E11), identify the personal pronouns and suggest what functions the different pronouns have (*Note*: -ya- in the verb word is an aspect marker which appears in the present tense when no complement follows the verb):

1. Umfana u-fana   ukudla
   boy   he-want food
   'The boy wants food'

2. U-fana   ukudla
   he-want food
   'He wants food'

3. uSipho yena u-fana   ukudla
   Sipho he   he-want food
   '_____ but Sipho (himself) wants food'

4. Yena u-fana   ukudla
   he   he-want food
   '_____ but he (himself) wants food'

5. Yena uSipho u-fana   ukudla
   he   Sipho he-want food
   '_____ but he, Sipho (himself), wants food'

6. U-shaya imbongolo
   he-hit   donkey
   'He hits a donkey'

7. U-shaya yona
   he-hit   it
   'He hits it'

8. U-ya-yi-shaya
   he- -it-hit
   'He hits it'

9. U-shaya yona imbongolo
   he-hit   it   donkey
   'He hits it, the donkey'

10. U-ya-yi-shaya yona
    he- -it-hit   it
    '_____ but he hits *it*'

11. U-ya-yi-shaya imbongolo
    he- -it-hit   donkey
    '_____ but he hits it, the donkey'

12. U-ya-yi-shaya yona imbongolo
    he- -it-hit   it   donkey
    '_____ but he hits *it*, the *donkey*'

6. Word structure

Morpheme

In considering data in previous chapters we have on a number of occasions been involved in identifying constituents of words (eg in Exercises 7–9). The implication of this procedure is that words may have an identifiable structure and be composed of smaller recurrent parts. There is a sense in which words are composed of sounds or letters, eg *cat* is composed of *c* + *a* + *t*; but such structure is not grammatical structure. We are concerned with the analysis of words into recurrent parts with an identifiable constant grammatical function or meaning. Such constituents of words are called 'morphemes'. We may, then, define a morpheme as "the minimal unit of grammar", and impose the condition that a morpheme must have a discernible meaning or function, which is more or less constant for all its occurrences in the structure of the words of a language.

Morphemes can be identified by comparing the words of a language which have a similar form. Recurrent sequences (of sounds or letters) with the same function or meaning are recognised as morphemes. Consider the following English examples:

refuse	dismiss	revive	refer
refus-al	dismiss-al	reviv-al	refer-al
refus-al-s	dismiss-al-s	reviv-al-s	refer-al-s

A comparison of these forms enables us to identify the following morphemes: *refuse*, *dismiss*, *revive*, *refer* with their usual dictionary meanings; *-al*, which has the function of deriving a noun from a verb; *-s*, which signals the grammatical category 'plural number'.

Now consider the following data (SIL 1980: A1) from Jebero (Peru):

1. nuŋʃa   'a little canoe'
2. nuŋʃawək   'my little canoe'
3. wilaʃa   'a little child'
4. tulapəŋ   'your leg'
5. piðəknəŋ   'his house'
6. piðəklusaʔ   'houses'
7. piðəkpəŋlusaʔ   'your houses'

By comparing Nos 1 and 3, we can recognise morphemes *nuŋ-* meaning 'canoe', *wila-* 'child', and *-ʃa* 'little' or 'diminutive' (cf *-let* in English *piglet*, *notelet*). Returning to No 2, we conclude that *-wək* is a morpheme meaning 'my', ie '1st person singular possessive'. Looking now at Nos 5 and 6, we can identify a morpheme *piðək-* meaning 'house', and conclude that *-nəŋ* is a morpheme meaning 'his' or '3rd person singular possessive', and *-lusaʔ* is a morpheme meaning 'plural'.

From No 7 we recognise a further morpheme *-pəŋ* meaning 'your' or '2nd person possessive'. Returning finally to No 4 we conclude that it is composed of the morpheme *tula-* meaning 'leg' and the '2nd person possessive' morpheme *-pəŋ*. A comparison of *-nəŋ* and *-pəŋ* might suggest a further subdivision into *-əŋ* 'possessive' and *-n/-p* '3rd person'/'2nd person'; but this analysis is contradicted by *-wək*, which cannot be analysed in this way: on the basis of the data given we are not justified in proposing a further analysis of *-nəŋ* and *-pəŋ*.

Summarising, the Jebero data contains the following morphemes:

Nouns: *nuŋ-* 'canoe', *piðək-* 'house', *tula-* 'leg', *wila-* 'child'.
Possessives: *-wək* '1st person singular', *-pəŋ* '2nd person', *-nəŋ* '3rd person singular'.
Number: *-lusaʔ* 'plural'.
Derivative: *-ʃa* 'diminutive'.

Root and affix

If you look back at the examples we have discussed, it is evident that a word is composed of a central morpheme, to which other morphemes are added. Semantically, the central morpheme carries the main lexical reference of the word, and the other morphemes modify that reference in various ways. So, for example, the English word *refusals* has *refuse* as its central morpheme, and the Jebero word *nuŋʃawək* has *nuŋ* as its central morpheme. The central morpheme is called the 'root' of the word, and the peripheral morphemes that are attached to the root are called 'affixes'.

Affixes are always 'bound' morphemes: they cannot occur alone as words, they occur only in combination with other morphemes. Thus in the English examples, *-al* and *-s* cannot be independent words, they are always bound to another morpheme. You will notice that in writing these morphemes, as indeed in writing many of the other morphemes we have identified in this and previous chapters, in fact all the bound morphemes, we have written them with a hyphen on the side or sides where they are bound. In the case of *-al* and *-s*, they are bound on the left, similarly all the bound affixes in the Jebero data; in Exercise 8, however, the Congo Swahili verb word has affix morphemes bound on the right.

Root morphemes may be bound or 'free', ie able to stand alone as an independent word. In the English data above, the roots *refuse*, *dismiss*, etc, are free morphemes, since they constitute words by themselves. Most roots in English are free. In the Jebero data it appears that the roots are bound; there is no example where a root stands alone, but it is not inconceivable, for example, that *nuŋ* might constitute an independent word in Jebero, with the meaning 'canoe', similarly *wila* 'child', *tula* 'leg', *piðək* 'house'. The limited data that we have does not allow us to definitely conclude this, although it could represent a reasonable hypothesis awaiting confirmation from further data. In the Congo Swahili data of Exercise 8, it seems fairly certain that the verb roots are bound, since they are preceded by at least a tense morpheme and a person morpheme functioning as subject.

Exercise 11

Identify the morphemes in the following Isthmus Zapotec (Mexico) data (SIL 1980: A5); list the morphemes with their meanings, and mark the bound morphemes with hyphens as appropriate:

1. ñee	'foot'	10. ʒigiluʔ	'your chin'
2. kañee	'feet'	11. kaʒigitu	'your(pl) chins'
3. ñeebe	'his foot'	12. kaʒigidu	'our chins'
4. ñeeluʔ	'your foot'	13. ʒike	'shoulder'
5. kañeetu	'your(pl) feet'	14. ʒikebe	'his shoulder'
6. kañeedu	'our feet'	15. kaʒikeluʔ	'your shoulders'
7. ʒigi	'chin'	16. diaga	'ear'
8. kaʒigi	'chins'	17. kadiagatu	'your(pl) ears'
9. ʒigibe	'his chin'	18. kadiagadu	'our ears'

Types of affix

In the examples we have been concerned with so far, we have come across two types of affix: those bound to the right (eg *ka-* 'plural' in the previous exercise); and those bound to the left (eg *-be* '3rd person singular masculine possessive' in the previous exercise). An affix which is bound to the right is called a 'prefix', and an affix which is bound to the left is called a 'suffix'. We introduced these terms informally in Chapter 3. Prefixes and suffixes are the most commonly occurring types of affix found in the world's languages, and in European languages they are probably the only regularly occurring affixes. But there are two further types of affix that are found less commonly: the 'infix' and the 'suprafix'.

An infix is an affix which interrupts the root; it is inserted into the root, instead of being joined at the side as with a prefix or suffix. Consider the following data (SIL 1980: A15) from Chontal of Oaxaca (Mexico):

1. tsetse	'squirrel'	tseɬtse	'squirrels'
2. tuwa	'foreigner'	tuɬwa	'foreigners'
3. teʔa	'elder'	teɬʔa	'elders'
4. mekoʔ	'spoon'	meɬkoʔ	'spoons'

The 'plural' morpheme is an infix *-ɬ-*, placed between the two syllables of the root morpheme.

Look now at the following Kamhmuʔ (Laos) data (SIL 1980: A16):

1. kap	'to grasp with tongs'	krnap	'tongs'
2. poot	'to walk on'	prnoot	'platform round a house'
3. sal	'to place in ear-lobe'	srnal	'ear ornament'
4. hiip	'to eat with a spoon'	hrniip	'spoon'

The morpheme *-rn-* is an infix, placed after the initial consonant of the root, with the function of deriving a noun from a verb; it might be called a 'nominaliser' morpheme.

The final affix type, the suprafix, is so called because it accompanies the root, and is usually written above the root. Suprafixes are, therefore, features of tone or stress or nasalisation, which have an identifiable meaning or grammatical function. This may be illustrated from English: the word *import* has two stress patternings associated with a difference of word-class membership. If *ímport* receives its main or primary stress on the first syllable, it belongs to the noun class; but if it receives its main stress on the second syllable—*impórt*—it belongs to the verb class. Arguably, therefore, the shift in stress patterning may be regarded as a morpheme (suprafix), since it has the same function as, for example, the suffix *-ment* in *statement* (verb → noun) or the prefix *be-* in *befriend* (noun → verb), depending on whether one takes *ímport* (noun) or *impórt* (verb) as the basic (root) morpheme.

Consider the following data (SIL 1980: A17) from Bekwarra (Nigeria). The language is tonal (ie pitch change on a word may signal a lexical/meaning difference), having a system of three tones: high tone is marked ´; low tone is marked `; mid tone is unmarked. Compare: *abe éfàà* 'they grind', *abe éfaà* 'they learn', *abe éfaa* 'they roast'.

1. abe éfàà   'they grind'
2. abe efàà   'they ground'
3. abe èfàà   'they should grind'
4. abe éhàrà   'they answer'
5. abe ehàrà   'they answered'
6. abe èhàrà   'they should answer'

The tone on the initial syllable of the root is a suprafix with a number of distinct meanings: high tone signals 'present tense'; mid tone signals 'past tense'; low tone signals 'obligation'.

Word structure

We have described the structure of words in terms of the constituent morphemes that compose words. For each word there is a root morpheme, to which may be added one or more affixes. A root morpheme is the minimal form of a word, and some words consist only of a root morpheme, eg *art*, *circle*, *difficult* in English. In some languages (eg Chinese or Vietnamese) the vast majority of words are of this kind; ie there are few if any affixes in these languages. In languages like English, words consisting of a single root morpheme occur freely, as well as words composed of a root and one or more affixes, eg *give-s*, *un-decide-d*, *stigmat-is(e)-ing*, *general-is(e)-ation-s*, *re-institut-ion-al-is(e)-ation*. In a language like Swahili probably the majority of words contain affixes attached to a root.

When multiple affixation occurs, it is usually the case that the affixes occur in a specific order, so that it is important in the description of word structure to state affix orders if this is appropriate. We have done this, for example, in the solutions to Exercises 9 and 11. Consider now the following data (SIL 1980: A11) from Sierra Popoluca (Mexico):

1. anʌkpa   'I go'
2. tanʌkgakpa   'You and I go again'
3. minʌktaʔmgakum   'You all went again'

4. nʌkjahpa   'They go'
5. nʌknejahum   'They have gone'
6. anʌknetaʔmgakum   'We (exclusive) have gone again'
7. nʌkjahgakpa   'They go again'
8. nʌkpa   'He goes'

Let us first of all identify the morphemes, and then establish the order of affixes. From its recurrence in all the eight examples, it would seem clear that *nʌk-* is the root morpheme meaning 'go'; it appears to be bound on the right (cf Nos 4, 5, 7, 8). Comparing Nos 1 and 4, which differ only in person, we conclude that *a-* is the '1st person singular' morpheme, and *-jah* the '3rd person plural' morpheme. A comparison of Nos 4 and 8 reveals that *-gak* means 'again' or 'iterative'. From No 2 we can now conclude that *ta-* means 'you and I' or '1st/2nd person singular'. What Nos 1, 2, 4, 7 and 8 have in common by contrast with the remainder is that they are present tense, which appears to be marked by *-pa*. If this is so, we conclude from No 8 that '3rd person singular' is unmarked. Nos 3, 5 and 6 contain the suffix *-um*, which appears to mean 'past tense'. Comparing Nos 3 and 6, we can conclude that *-taʔm* means 'plural (for 1st/2nd person)', while *mi-* is the morpheme for '2nd person'; we must revise our assessment of *a-* to '1st person', being singular in No 1 without *-taʔm*, but becoming plural in No 6 only by the presence of *-taʔm*. The remaining morpheme to be identified is *-ne* in Nos 5 and 6, which corresponds to *have* in the English gloss, ie it has the meaning 'perfective'.

Summarising, we have identified the following morphemes in the verb word in Sierra Popoluca:

Verb Root: *nʌk-* 'go'.
Person Affix: *a-* '1st person', *mi-* '2nd person', *ta-* '1st/2nd person', *-jah* '3rd person plural'.
Tense Affix: *-pa* 'present', *-um* 'past'.
Aspect Affix: *-gak* 'iterative', *-ne* 'perfective'.
Number Affix: *-taʔm* 'plural'.

The order of morphemes is as follows:

Person (1st–2nd)—Root—Perfective—Plural/3rd person plural—Iterative—Tense.

Root and stem

We have identified the root as the part of a word to which affixes are added. Alternatively, the root may be viewed as the part of a word that remains after all the affixes have been removed. What we need in addition to the terms 'root' and 'affix' is a term to designate a structure (word) composed of root plus affix(es), but which may itself be further affixed. The term used is 'stem'. A stem is a word which may still have additional affixes attached to it. The term 'stem' thus includes 'root': a root is a minimal stem. Look at the following English example:

re-align-ment-s
ROOT
–STEM–
——STEM——

Align is the root. It is prefixed by *re-*, and *realign* is a stem, since it may be further affixed, eg by *-ment*. *Realignment* is also a stem, since it may be affixed by the 'plural' morpheme *-s*. However, *realignments* is no longer a stem, since it may not take any further affixes.

Exercise 12

Identify the morphemes in the following data (SIL 1980: A19) from Chatino (Mexico), and list them with their meanings (*Notes*: treat *ngu-* as a single morpheme; ~ marks nasalisation):

1.	ngudaõ	'we(inclusive) gave'
2.	ndaõ	'we(inclusive) give'
3.	ngudaba	'we(exclusive) gave'
4.	ngudã	'I gave'
5.	nguda	'You/he gave'
6.	nda	'You/he give'
7.	ndja	'You/he pay' (ie are caused to give)
8.	ngudja	'You/he paid'
9.	kuda	'You/he will give'
10.	kusiʔju	'You/he will cut'
11.	nsiʔjū	'I cut (present)'
12.	nsjiʔju	'You/he are caused to cut'
13.	ngusiʔjuõ	'We(inclusive) cut (past)'
14.	ngusiʔjuwõ	'You(plural) cut (past)'
15.	ngusjiʔju	'You/he were caused to cut'

7. Combining morphemes

Derivation and inflection

In the previous chapter we considered the decomposition of words into their constituent parts, ie morphemes. That is to say, we took an analytical aproach to the consideration of word structure. In this chapter we are going to take a 'synthetic' approach, attempting to answer the questions: "How do morphemes combine together to form words?", "What kinds of processes are at work?"

We need first of all to notice that two general processes are at work in combining morphemes into words: 'derivation' and 'inflection'. Derivation is a lexical process which forms a new word out of an existing word by the addition of a morpheme. For example, in English the suffix *-ment* may be added to the verb *state* to derive the noun *statement*, which is a different word, an additional vocabulary item in English. Similarly in the Kamhmu? examples cited in the previous chapter, the addition of the infix *-rn-* to, say, the verb *poot* 'to walk on' derives a noun *prnoot* 'platform around a house', an additional lexical item in this language. Strictly speaking, the term 'derivation' refers to the creation of a new word by means of the addition of an affix to a stem; but we shall also be considering other word-formation processes in this chapter, which have a similar, lexical, function.

The other general process at work in combining morphemes, inflection, is a grammatical process. For example, the plural morpheme in English is an inflectional morpheme. Inflections represent alternative grammatical forms of a word. The plural form *boys*, for instance, does not represent a different lexical item from the singular form *boy*, but rather merely the addition of the morphemic realisation of the grammatical category of plural number. An inflectional morpheme, then, does not derive a different vocabulary item; it realises alternative grammatical forms of the same word.

The distinction between derivation and inflection is a morphological one. It should not be concluded that a particular meaning (eg 'plural') is universally represented either inflectionally or derivationally. Plural number, for example, may be marked equally well by quantifiers (eg *many*, *several*) or numerals, ie lexically, as by an inflectional affix. Similarly, 'person' may be realised by an affix in the verb word (ie inflectionally) or alternatively by a separate pronoun word (ie lexically); compare the distinction made in Chapter 5 between bound and free pronouns. Or consider the Sierra Popoluca data in the previous chapter: here the meaning 'iterative' is realised grammatically by the inflectional morpheme *-gak*, whereas in English this meaning is realised lexically by the separate word *again*. The term 'derivational' and 'inflectional' are, then, a means of distinguishing a morphological process that creates new vocabulary items on the one hand, and on the other a morphological process that realises alternative grammatical forms of the same word.

Compounding

We look first under the broad heading of derivation at a word-formation process known as 'compounding'. Compounding involves the combination of two roots (Root + Root), to form a new word or stem. For example, in English the word *driftwood* is made up of two roots, the verb *drift* and the noun *wood*, both of which may be independent words in their own right. Similarly in German, the word *Lebensabend* 'old age' is a compound of the nouns *Leben* 'life' and *Abend* 'evening'.

In compounding, two roots combine in such a way that each loses its independent word status and the new combination takes on the characteristics of a single word. These single-word characteristics may include the semantic dimension, eg a compound may have a unitary meaning not immediately derivable from its elements, as in German *Augenblick* 'moment', made up of *Auge* 'eye' and *Blick* 'look/glance'. Or they may include the grammatical dimension, eg a compound will inflect like a single word, as English *babysit*. This has all the usual verb inflections of English, eg *babysits*, *babysitting*, *babysat*; but the *baby* part of the compound does not inflect, eg for 'plural', however many babies may be involved. Additionally, single-word characteristics may include the phonological dimension, eg a compound will take on the stress features of single words, or regular phonological changes may occur when roots are compounded. In English, for example, single words have characteristically one primary (or main), stress, so that in a compound one of the roots normally loses its primary stress; compare "a bláck boárd" and "a bláckboard". In German, a number of roots forming the first element of a compound regularly take an additional -s, eg *Universitätsprofessor* 'university professor', *Universitätsgebäude* 'university building', *Universitätsstudium* 'study at a university'.

Consider now the following data (SIL 1980: 18) from Igede (Nigeria):

1. iyo	'meat'	enyi	'water'	iyenyi	'fish'
2. imi	'hunger'	enyi	'water'	imenyi	'thirst'
3. ube	'room'	utoji	'medicine'	ubutoji	'clinic'.

It will be noticed that all the nouns in this data begin with a vowel and end with a vowel. However, it appears that two vowels cannot occur together in a word, so that on compounding the final vowel of the first element is omitted. Note that in the compounds in this data it is the first element that is semantically primary, ie *iyenyi* 'fish' is a kind of meat (*iyo*), *imenyi* 'thirst' is a kind of 'hunger' (*imi*), and *ubutoji* 'clinic' is a kind of 'room' (*ube*). In our English and German examples, representative of these languages generally, the order is reversed: *driftwood* is a kind of 'wood', *Universitätsgebäude* is a kind of *Gebäude* 'building'.

Compounding is not always a matter of the combination of two roots. Take the compound *watchmaker* in English, representative of a common type of English compound. This is a combination of the noun root *watch* and the derived noun *maker*, which has a verb root *make*. But there is no *watchmake* in English, so that the second element of *watchmaker* is not, strictly speaking, a root, but a stem. Compounds themselves should also be regarded as stems, since they may be affixed; eg *watchmakers* by the 'plural' *-s* suffix, *overtaker* by the 'nominaliser' *-er* suffix. Indeed, compounds may be elements in further compounds, eg in German *Mitunterschrift* 'joint signature', made up of *mit* 'with' plus *Unterschrift* 'signature', which in turn is a compound made up of *unter* 'under' plus *Schrift* 'writing'.

Exercise 13

Examine the following data (SIL 1980: I9) from Mbembe (Nigeria) and say what phonological processes occur as a result of compounding:

1. ana	'oil'	ɛpya	'market'	ɛnapya	'selling of oil'
2. ɔbɔːk	'arm'	ɛdɔŋɔ	'throat'	ɛbɔːdɔŋɔ	'wrist'
3. ɔsɔːm	'house'	ɛmma	'mouth'	ɛsɔːmma	'threshold'
4. eci	'tree'	ɛraŋa	'root'	ɛciraŋa	'medicine'
5. ɛciraŋa	'medicine'	ɔsɔːm	'house'	ɔciraŋasɔːm	'hospital'
6. eci	'tree'	ikwuma	'half'	icikwuma	'log of wood'
7. ɔda	'sleep'	icen	'eye'	idacen	'dream'
8. ɛba	'breast'	asi	'liquid'	abasi	'milk'

Derivation

We look secondly at derivation proper, the coining of new items of vocabulary by means of affixation. All four types of affix may be used derivationally. We mentioned a derivational suffix and a derivational infix at the beginning of the chapter. A derivational prefix can be illustrated from English, eg *be-* in *befriend*, deriving a verb from the noun *friend*. The stress change on the English word *import*, deriving a noun from a verb or vice versa, could be regarded as a derivational suprafix. Derivation involves the addition of an affix to a root or stem to form a different lexical item (word or new stem).

The majority of derivational affixes effect a change in the word class membership of the stem to which they are added, ie the derived word (or stem) has a different word class membership from that of the stem being affixed. For example, in German the addition of the suffix *-heit* to the adjective *wahr* 'true' derives the noun *Wahrheit* 'truth', in English the addition of the prefix *en-* to the adjective *large* derives the verb *enlarge*. A derivational affix may not in some cases effect a change in the word class membership of the stem to which it is added, eg in English the negative prefix *un-* when added to the adjective *true* derives another adjective *untrue*, and when added to the verb *tie* derives another verb *untie*. Intermediate between these two types of derivational affix is a third type which does not effect a change of word class, but of sub-class within a class, eg in English there are several derivational suffixes forming abstract nouns from concrete nouns: *machine-ery*, *boy-hood*, *dictator-ship*.

Consider now the following data (SIL 1980: I2) from Mbembe (Nigeria):

1. bèŋa	'to grow'	àbèŋíjí	'growth'
2. ɓɔr	'to be pale'	àɓɔríjí	'paleness'
3. dòŋ	'to be deep'	àdòŋíjí	'depth'

4. gòrɔ	'to be proud'	àgòríjí	'pride'
5. báŋ	'to be dirty'	ábáɲíjí	'dirtiness'
6. cámɛ	'to be small'	ácámíjí	'smallness'

In this data, the derivation of a noun from a verb involves a simultaneous prefix-ation and suffixation. Prefixation is by *a-* which 'agrees' in tone with the root, low tone before low tone (Nos 1–4), high tone before high tone (Nos 5 and 6). Suffix-ation is by *-íjí*. If the verb root ends in a vowel (Nos 1, 4 and 6), this is deleted when *-íjí* is affixed.

Even more true of derivation than of compounding is the possibility of a word resulting from the application of several derivational processes. We noted this point in the previous chapter. For example, the English word *intermarriage* may be viewed as the prefixation of the verb root *marry* by *inter-* (which does not change the word class), and then suffixation by *-age* to derive a noun. Similarly, the German word *misstönig* is first of all the prefixation of the noun root *Ton* 'sound' by *miss-* to derive *Misston* 'dissonance' (still a noun), and the suffixation of this stem by *-ig* accompanied by umlaut of the root vowel to derive the adjective *mis-stönig* 'dissonant'.

Exercise 14

Examine the following Lisu (North Thailand) data (SIL 1980: I3) and identify the deriv-ational affixes, giving each a 'meaning'.

1. syɨ	'to sweep'	9. tshɨ	'to wash'
2. syɨdwu	'broom'	10. tshɨswu	'washer woman'
3. syɨswu	'sweeper'	11. tshɨgwu	'washing place'
4. tshye	'to hide'	12. tshɨdwu	'thing for washing clothes'
5. tshyegwu	'hiding place'	13. pū	'to write'
6. tya	'to live'	14. pūdwu	'pencil'
7. tyaswu	'inhabitant'	15. pūswu	'writer'
8. tyagwu	'house'		

Other word-formation processes

Apart from the non-morphological ways of adding new vocabulary to a language such as borrowing words from other languages (cf *detente* in English from French, or *le weekend* in French from English) or creating words from roots in classical Latin and Greek (eg many scientific and medical terms), there are a few more strictly morphological ways of forming new words, but of a minor nature by comparison with compounding and derivation proper.

Perhaps the most widespread of these minor word-formation processes is one known as 'conversion', which could be described as derivation without affixation. A word (or stem) belonging to one word class is transferred to another word class without any change of form by means of affixation. For example, the word *bottle* in English is a noun, but it is also used as a verb without any change of form, except that as a verb it is subject to the usual inflectional affixation of verbs (*he/she bottles, bottling, bottled*). Compare also: *peel* (noun and verb), *race* (verb and noun), *dirty* (adjective and verb), *escape* (verb and noun), *picture* (noun and verb). Similarly in other languages, eg French *travail/travailler* 'work', *lutte/lutter* 'fight' (noun and verb, the *-er* being the verb inflectional suffix for the infinitive, ie citation form), *innocent* 'innocent' (adjective and noun) together with the verb *innocenter* 'to declare innocent'; also German *Blick/blicken* 'look, glance', *Arbeit/arbeiten* 'work', *Rauch/rauchen* 'smoke' (all noun and verb, with *-en* the inflectional suffix for the infinitive form of the verb).

A second minor word-formation process is one known as 'back-formation', which is in a way the converse of derivation: a word is coined by the removal of a (supposed) affix. For example, the verb *babysit* in English was derived from the noun *babysitter* by the removal of the *-er*, which was associated with the 'agentive' suffix of words like *walker*, *seller*, *flyer*, etc. The verb *edit* was derived from the noun *editor* in a similar way. Unlike derivation proper, however, the process of back-formation is not obvious to the modern native-speaker without access to historical linguistic information. Nevertheless, back-formation is a process by which new words may yet be coined in a contemporary language.

A last minor word-formation process that we might mention is the coining of new words by forming acronyms, ie taking the initial letters of the words in a phrase and forming them into a new word. For example, the word *radar* was formed in this way, standing for 'radio detecting and ranging'; also *laser*, 'lightwave amplification by stimulated emission of radiation'. But this word-formation process is popular with international organisations, cf *NATO* 'North Atlantic Treaty Organisation', *UNESCO* 'United Nations Educational, Scientific and Cultural Organisation'.

Inflection

We come finally in this chapter to inflectional morphemes, those which add grammatical meaning to a word. Inflectional morphemes cannot change the word class membership of a stem to which they are affixed. They realise grammatical categories and produce different grammatical forms of the same word. Take the verb in English: as a rule, it has potentially five different forms—base form/present tense (eg *show*), 3rd person singular present tense (eg *shows*), past tense (eg *showed*), present participle (eg *showing*), past participle (eg *shown*). In fact, for the majority of verbs the past tense and the past participle have the same form (eg *walked*). The inflectional morphemes here realise categories like person/tense (*-s*), past tense (*-ed*), and participles (*-ing*, *-n*); and the resulting verb word forms are used appropriately in specific lexical and syntactic contexts, eg the present participle is used with *be* to realise 'progressive aspect' ("they are *showing*") or after certain other verbs ("they like *reading* stories").

In English, inflectional morphemes are always suffixes (cf also 'plural' and 'possessive' in the noun—*girls*, *girl's*); but any of the four types of affix may be inflectional. In the Congo Swahili data of Exercise 8, the inflections for person and tense are both prefixes, eg *ninasem* 'I speak' (*ni-* '1st person singular', *na-* 'present tense'). In the previous chapter, one of the illustrations of an infix was the inflectional morpheme 'plural' in Chontal of Oaxaca, eg *tułwa* 'foreigners' (*-ł-* 'plural'). And in the

Chatino data of Exercise 12, the inflectional morpheme '1st person singular' is a suprafix of nasalisation, eg *ngudā* 'I gave' (*ngu-* 'past tense', *-da* 'give', ~ '1st person singular').

We have noted on a number of occasions that grammatical categories intersect and find a realisation by a common morpheme; for example, number and person intersect in pronouns; tense, person and number intersect in verbs. That is to say, one inflectional affix may 'carry' a number of grammatical meanings, and it is not possible to identify a separate segment of the word for each meaning. For example, the *-s* inflection in the English verb (eg *shows*) 'carries' the meanings '3rd person', 'singular number', and 'present tense'. This point can perhaps be illustrated best from the conjugational and declensional paradigms of Latin or Greek grammar. Consider, for instance, the verb form *amo* 'I love' in Latin. It is composed of the root *am-* 'to love' and the inflectional suffix *-o*, meaning '1st person singular present active indicative'; ie it 'carries' five meanings. It is '1st person' by contrast with, say, '2nd person', eg *amas* 'you love'. It is 'singular' in number by contrast with 'plural', eg *amamus* 'we love'. It is 'present' in tense by contrast with, say, 'past', eg *amabam* 'I loved'. It is 'active' in voice by contrast with 'passive', eg *amor* 'I am loved'. And it is 'indicative' in mood by contrast with, say, 'subjunctive', eg *amarem* 'I should love'. Thus, there is no necessary one-to-one relationship between inflectional affix and grammatical category or meaning.

Exercise 15

Identify the morphemes in the following Sierra Aztec (Mexico) data (SIL 1980: A9) and list them with their meanings. Say if the affixes are inflectional or derivational. Chart the order of morphemes.

1.	nimitsita	'I see you'
2.	nikita	'I see him'
3.	nikmaka	'I give it to him'
4.	tikmaka	'You give it to him'
5.	tinetʃita	'You see me'
6.	nannetʃmaka	'You(pl) give it to me'
7.	tikonmaka	'You give it to him, Sir'
8.	tikonitatihtsinoh	'You see him, most honoured Sir'
9.	tinetʃonita	'You see me, Sir'
10.	tinetʃonmakatihtsinoh	'You give it to me, most honoured Sir'
11.	nannetʃonmakatsikah	'You(pl) give it to me, honoured Sirs'
12.	nannetʃonitatihtsinoh	'You(pl) see me, most honoured Sirs'
13.	tinetʃonitatsikah	'You see me, honoured Sir'
14.	nannetʃonmakatihtsinoh	'You(pl) give it to me, most honoured Sirs'

8. Morpheme variants

Some knowledge of phonetics is assumed in this chapter.

Allomorphs

In Chapter 3 the reader was requested to note the different pronunciations of the 'plural' suffix in the English words *apples*, *apricots* and *peaches*. We come now to consider the nature of such differences. What differences like this mean is that a particular morpheme (eg 'plural number') may not be always pronounced (or spelt) in the same way wherever it occurs as a constituent of a word. Morphemes, that is to say, may have variant realisations (pronunciations or spellings), depending on their context of occurrence. These variant realisations are known as 'allomorphs'. From our examples above, the English 'plural' morpheme has the allomorphs /z/, /s/ and /ɪz/ respectively. Strictly speaking, then, the 'morpheme' is an abstract unit, whose concrete realisation in sound or spelling is by means of a 'morph' or—if there are variant realisations—'allomorphs'. We can equate the term 'morpheme' with the 'meaning' or 'function', and the term 'morph' with sounds or letters.

Some morphemes have only a single realisation; they always appear with the same pronunciation/spelling in a particular variety of the language (eg dialect or accent). For example, the 'present participle' morpheme in standard English has the single realisation *-ing*/ɪŋ/in all its contexts of occurrence, ie whichever verb root it is affixed to (cf *sowing*, *sleeping*, *finding*). Most inflectional morphemes in English, however, do have alternative realisations (allomorphs), such as the 'plural' inflection. But it is not only inflectional morphemes that may have allomorphs; derivational morphemes and root morphemes may also have variant forms. For example, the 'negative' prefix *un-* has variant forms in *unpleasant*/ʌm/, *unkind*/ʌŋ/ and *unchanged*/ʌn/; the root *resign* has variant forms in *resigns*/rīzaīn/and *resignation*/rezīgn/.

There are two kinds of descriptive explanation for morpheme variants. On the one hand, the pronunciation of a morpheme may vary because of its phonological context, ie the nature of the sounds in the accompanying morpheme(s): such allomorphs are said to be 'phonologically conditioned'. On the other hand, the realisation of a morpheme may vary quite arbitrarily when combined with certain other morphemes: such variation is said to be 'morphologically conditioned', ie the variation depends purely on which morpheme accompanies that with variant forms, but not on its phonological form.

Exercise 16

Identify the variant forms (allomorphs) of the 'past tense' morpheme in the following English data. Be sure to consider the pronunciation:

1. believe	believed	6. miss	missed
2. float	floated	7. redeem	redeemed
3. snatch	snatched	8. give	gave
4. allow	allowed	9. catch	caught
5. need	needed	10. put	put

Phonological conditioning

The allomorphs of a morpheme are said to be phonologically conditioned when the variation in pronunciation can be explained from the phonological context, ie the sounds composing the adjoining morph(s). Take the allomorphs of the 'plural' morpheme in English, with which we began this chapter: /z/, /s/, /ɪz/. These allomorphs are phonologically conditioned: which one of them occurs depends on the nature of the final sound of the noun stem to which the 'plural' morpheme is affixed. If the final sound of the noun stem is a sibilant (ie/s, z, ʃ, ʒ, tʃ, dʒ/), then the 'plural' morpheme is realised by the allomorph /ɪz/; if the stem-final sound is a voiceless consonant (other than a sibilant), the allomorph is /s/; if the stem-final sound is a voiced sound, ie a vowel or a voiced consonant (other than a sibilant), then the allomorph of the 'plural' is /z/.

This conditioning just described may be expressed in the following formula:

{plural} →
/ɪz/   after stem-final sibilants
/s/   after-stem-final voiceless consonants
/z/   elsewhere

The morpheme is conventionally written in curly brackets (braces), and the allomorphs in the slashed brackets of phonemic transcription. The arrow represents the statement "is realised by the allomorphs", and the contexts of conditioning are put after each allomorph. Note that the allomorph with the narrowest distribution (ie occurring after the least number of sounds) is put first, and that with the widest distribution last. Each successive conditioning statement excludes the one(s) that have preceded, so that the last one is appropriately expressed by an "elsewhere" statement, since it refers to every phonological environment not previously mentioned. A similar statement can be made for the 'past tense' suffix identified in Exercise 16:

{past tense} →
/ɪd/   after stem-final alveolar plosives
/t/   after stem-final voiceless consonants
/d/   elsewhere

Phonological conditioning, thus, implies providing a plausible phonological explanation from surrounding context for allomorphic variation. Consider now the following data (SIL 1980: H10) from Ilocano (Philippines):

1. tugawko	'my chair'	7. bagasko	'my rice'
2. tugawmo	'your chair'	8. bagasmo	'your rice'
3. tugawna	'his chair'	9. bagasna	'his rice'
4. sabak	'my banana'	10. sidak	'my food'
5. sabam	'your banana'	11. sidam	'your food'
6. sabana	'his banana'	12. sidana	'his food'

The nouns in this data are composed of a root followed by a 'possessive' suffix. Three possessive morphemes are represented in this data: '1st person singular', '2nd person', '3rd person singular masculine'. The '3rd person singular masculine possessive' morpheme is realised by a single morph /-na/ (Nos 3, 6, 9, 12). The other two possessive morphemes are each realised by two allomorphs, the '1st person singular possessive' by /-ko/ and /-k/, and the '2nd person possessive' by /-mo/ and /-m/. The allomorphs of both morphemes are phonologically conditioned in the same way: /-ko/ and /-mo/ occur after a root-final consonant, while /-k/ and /-m/ occur after a root-final vowel. A statement for the '1st person singular possessive' would be as follows:

$$\left\{ \begin{array}{c} \text{1st person} \\ \text{singular possessive} \end{array} \right\} \rightarrow \begin{array}{ll} /k/ & \text{after root-final vowel} \\ /ko/ & \text{elsewhere} \end{array}$$

And similarly for the '2nd person possessive':

$$\left\{ \begin{array}{c} \text{2nd person} \\ \text{possessive} \end{array} \right\} \rightarrow \begin{array}{ll} /m/ & \text{after root-final vowel} \\ /mo/ & \text{elsewhere} \end{array}$$

Exercise 17

Identify the allomorphs of the 'plural' and '2nd person possessive' morphemes in the following Turkish data (SIL 1980: H12), and state the phonological conditioning. (*Note*: the answer lies in the vowels.)

		plural	'your' + sing noun	'your' + pl noun
1. mum	'candle'	mumlar	mumun	mumlarɪn
2. kibrit	'match'	kibritler	kibritin	kibritlerin
3. yzym	'grape'	yzymler	yzymyn	yzymlerin
4. sɪnɪf	'class'	sɪnɪflar	sɪnɪfɪn	sɪnɪflarɪn
5. ders	'lesson'	dersler	dersin	derslerin
6. satʃ	'hair'	satʃlar	satʃin	satʃlarɪn
7. gøz	'eye'	gøzler	gøzyn	gøzlerin
8. top	'gun'	toplar	topun	toplarɪn
9. kuʃ	'bird'	kuʃlar	kuʃun	kuʃlarɪn
10. diʃ	'tooth'	diʃler	diʃin	diʃlerin
11. ok	'arrow'	oklar	okun	oklarɪn
12. køk	'root'	køkler	køkyn	køklerin

Morphological conditioning

Allomorphs of a morpheme, whose variation cannot be accounted for phonologically, are said to be 'morphologically conditioned'. That is to say, a particular allomorph of a morpheme occurs with an arbitrary set of other morphemes; the presence of one of that set determines or conditions the occurrence of the particular allomorph. For example, the allomorphs of the 'plural' morpheme in German, which we discussed in Chapter 3, are morphologically conditioned allomorphs: -e/ə/ occurs with noun morphemes like *Tag* 'day', *Mond* 'moon', *Schuh* 'shoe', etc., -er /ər/ occurs with noun morphemes like *Ei* 'egg', *Kind* 'child', *Licht* 'light', etc, and so on. Learners of German know that for each noun learnt as a vocabulary item they must also learn which plural allomorph it is associated with; apart from a few rules of thumb (eg feminine nouns ending in *e* usually take plural in -*n*), there is no general predictability, and certainly not of a phonological nature.

A similar kind of statement of allomorphic variation can be made for morphologically conditioned allomorphs as for phonologically conditioned ones, except that in the case of morphological conditioning a list of possible accompanying morphemes must be provided for each allomorph, rather than a general statement of conditioning. A statement for the 'plural' morpheme in German would have the following kind of form:

{plural} →   /s/   with the following noun stems:
            Detail 'detail', *Hotel* 'hotel', *Team* 'team', etc
      /əʳ/   with the following noun stems:
            Brett 'board', *Kleid* 'dress', *Leib* 'body', etc
      /ø/   with the following noun stems:
            Haken 'hook', *Koffer* 'case', *Fenster* 'window', etc
    /(ə)n/   with the following noun stems:
            Biene 'bee', *Frau* 'woman', *Vetter* 'cousin', etc
      /ə/   elsewhere, ie with the following noun stems:
            Erfolg 'success', *Hund* 'dog', *Dieb* 'thief', etc

To avoid over-complicating this statement, no account has been taken of the operation of 'umlaut' on stem vowels with some of these suffixes in respect of specific noun stems.

Consider now the following data (SIL 1980: H2) from Hixkaryana (Brazil):

	Verb stem	Adjective	
1.	tawa-	tawanje	'dark'
2.	tak-	takdje	'warm'
3.	bata-	bataʃe	'rotten'
4.	tak-	takrje	'wet'
5.	tawas-	tawasdje	'light'
6.	tutʃu-	tutʃurje	'red'
7.	tatʃenot-	tatʃenotdje	'cold'

In this data, the 'adjectiviser' morpheme has four allomorphs, which are morphologically conditioned as follows:

{adjectiviser} →   /nje/   with the following verb stem:
                    tawa-
            /ʃe/   with the following verb stem:
                    bata-
           /rje/   with the following verb stems:
                    tak-, *tutʃu-*
           /dje/   elsewhere, ie with the following verb
                    stems: *tak-*, *tatʃenot-*, *tawas-*

Exercise 18

Identify the morphemes in the following Isthmus Zapotec (Mexico) data (SIL 1980: H5), and describe the allomorphs of the tense morphemes.

1. rukaadu	'we write'	14. ruyubibe	'he looks for'
2. rukaabe	'he writes'	15. zuyubibe	'he will look for'
3. zukaabe	'he will write'	16. biyubibe	'he looked for'
4. bikaabe	'he wrote'	17. kuyubibe	'he is looking for'
5. kukaabe	'he is writing'	18. rireebe	'he goes out'
6. ruzooñebe	'he runs'	19. zareebe	'he will go out'
7. zuzooñebe	'he will run'	20. bireebe	'he went out'
8. bizooñebe	'he ran'	21. kareebe	'he is going out'
9. kuzooñebe	'he is running'	22. ribanibe	'he wakes up'
10. ridʒelabe	'he finds'	23. zabanibe	'he will wake up'
11. zadʒelabe	'he will find'	24. bibanibe	'he woke up'
12. bidʒelabe	'he found'	25. kabanibe	'he is waking up'
13. kadʒelabe	'he is finding'	26. kabanidu	'we are waking up'

Mixed conditioning

Sometimes the allomorphs of a morpheme cannot be accounted for completely by either phonological conditioning or morphological conditioning alone; some of the allomorphs are found to be phonologically conditioned and some morphologically conditioned. This is, in fact, the case with the allomorphs of the 'plural' morpheme and of the 'past tense' morpheme in English. In our previous discussions of these morphemes we have considered only the 'regular' forms, ie /s/, /z/, /ɪz/ for 'plural' and /t/, /d/, /ɪd/ for 'past tense' (but cf Exercise 16). Consider, however, the following plurals of English nouns: *deer, mice, oxen, teeth, criteria*. The allomorph of the 'plural' in *deer* is zero /ø/, ie there is no visible or audible mark of plurality; in *mice* the allomorph is the stem vowel change /aʊ → aɪ/; in *oxen* it is the suffix /ən/; in *teeth* it is the stem vowel change /u → i) and in *criteria* it is the change taken over from Latin from /ən/ (*criterion* /kraɪtɪərɪən/) to /ə/ (/kraɪtɪərɪə/), ie in effect the loss of final /n/. These allomorphs are all morphologically conditioned; they apply to only a small number of noun stems, and there are more of a similar kind. Clearly, then, the allomorphs of the 'plural' morpheme in English represent an instance of mixed conditioning.

In making a statement of mixed conditioning, since the general principle is that allomorphs with the most restricted distribution are listed first and in mixed conditioning the phonologically conditioned allomorphs generally have the wider distribution, those that are morphologically conditioned are stated first. For example, a statement of the variants of the 'plural' morpheme in English would have the following kind of form:

{plural} →

/ən/	with the following noun stems: *ox, child*
/ø/	with the following noun stems: *deer, sheep*, etc
/aʊ→aɪ/	with the following noun stems: *mouse, louse*, etc
/u→i/	with the following noun stems: *tooth, goose*, etc
/ən→ə/	with the following noun stems: *criterion, phenomenon*, etc

/īz/   after stem-final sibilants
/s/   after stem-final voiceless consonants
/z/   elsewhere

Now consider the following Northern Tepehuan (Mexico) data (SIL 1980: H19):

	Singular	Plural
1. 'rabbit'	toʃi	totoʃi
2. 'man'	kʌli	kʌkʌli
3. 'foreigner'	obai	obai
4. 'tree'	uʃi	uʃi
5. 'son'	mara	mamara
6. 'stone'	obai	oxodai
7. 'friend'	aduni	aaduni
8. 'arrow'	uyi	uxuyi
9. 'turkey'	tova	totova
10. 'older brother'	ʃiʌgi	ʃiʃiʌgi
11. 'species of bird'	adatomali	aadatomali
12. 'needle'	oyi	oxoyi
13. 'younger brother'	sukuli	susukuli
14. 'species of fish'	aaʃi	aaʃi
15. 'rat'	dʌgi	dʌdʌgi
16. 'water jar'	ayi	axayi

There are three allomorphs of the 'plural' morpheme in this data. The allomorph with the widest distribution is the reduplication of the initial syllable (consisting of a Consonant + Vowel or just of a Vowel, ie/(C)V/), Nos 1, 2, 5, 7, 9, 10, 11, 13, 15: this allomorph can be regarded as phonologically conditioned. The one with the next widest distribution is the reduplication of the initial syllable consisting of just a Vowel with the addition of the consonant /x/, ie /Vx/: this must be regarded as morphologically conditioned, since the same initial vowel occurs as in the regular allomorph, viz /a/, cf Nos 7/14 with 16. The third allomorph is /ø/, Nos 3, 4 and 14, which must also be regarded as morphologically conditioned. Our statement for the 'plural' morpheme in this data might, then, be as follows:

{plural} →   /ø/   with the following noun stems: *obai* 'foreigner', *uʃi* 'tree', *aaʃi* 'species of fish'
     /Vx/   with the following noun stems: *odai* 'stone', *uyi* 'arrow', *oyi* 'needle', *ayi* 'water jar'
/(C)V/   elsewhere

Exercise 19

Make a statement for the '3rd person singular masculine possessive' (*his*) and the '3rd person singular masculine reflexive possessive' (*his own*) morphemes in the following data (SIL 1980: H20) based on *Kaiwa* (Brazil).

1. iñãka	'his head'	oãka	'his own head'
2. inambi	'his ear'	onambi	'his own ear'
3. ipo	'his hand'	opo	'his own hand'
4. ijavati	'his corn'	oavati	'his own corn'
5. ijɨbɨ	'his land'	oɨbɨ	'his own land'

6. iñãpeku   'his tongue'   oãpeku   'his own tongue'
7. hiʔi   'his water'   oʔi   'his own water'
8. hiʔabɨ   'his hair'   oʔabɨ   'his own hair'
9. iñãmba   'his place'   oãmba   'his own place'
10. ijape   'his shell'   oape   'his own shell'
11. ijagwa   'his dog'   ojagwa   'his own dog'
12. ijape   'his track'   gwape   'his own track'
13. ijupa   'his lying place'   gwupa   'his own lying place'
14. iñãta   'his home'   ŋwãta   'his own home'
15. iñẽmbiʔu   'his food'   ŋwẽmbiʔu   'his own food'
16. ijɨvɨrɨ   'his younger brother'   gwɨvɨrɨ   'his own younger brother'
17. hiʔaŋgwe   'his shadow'   gwʔaŋgwe   'his own shadow'

9. What is a word?

'Word' an ambiguous term

Within linguistics, as indeed within ordinary language, the term 'word' is multiply ambiguous. We use it to refer to different kinds of unit. For example, I might say that this sentence contains eleven words. By 'word' here I would mean blocks of letters separated by spaces. A dictionary will claim to contain "15,000 words", and the term has changed its reference: for example, the items *sing*, *sings*, *singing*, *sang* and *sung* will count as only one of the 15,000 'words' in the dictionary. Or consider the case of 'homonyms', either spelt the same (ie 'homographs') or pronounced the same (ie 'homophones'); for example, *long* (opposite of *short*) and *long* ('desire strongly') are homonyms (both homographs and homophones), *bow* (as in "bow and arrow") and *bow* ('inclination of the head') are homographs but pronounced differently, while *bow* ('inclination of the head') and *bough* are homophones but not homographs. In each of these cases, we may ask whether they are the same word, and the answer will depend on the point of view that we take.

If we take the point of view of the written language, regarding words as combinations of letters (the 'orthographic' point of view), then *row* (ie $r + o + w$) represents one word, however many 'meanings' it might have. Similarly, from the point of view of pronunciation ('phonological'), regarding words as combinations of sounds (phonemes), then /baʊ/ (ie /b/ + /ɑ/ + /ʊ/) represents one word, however many spellings or meanings it might have. From the point of view of the dictionary, however, every item with a 'different meaning' (though that is open to interpretation) is a different word; so that *bow* (as in "bow and arrow"), *bow* ('inclination of the head') and *bough* are all separate words, as indeed are *bow* ('inclination of the head'—noun) and *bow* ('incline the head'—verb). However, as we noted earlier, *bows*, *bowing* and *bowed* would not be separate words in the dictionary, but regarded as 'forms' of the word *bow* (verb). Clearly, then, we need some new terminology to enable us to make the necessary distinctions that we have been discussing.

Word-forms

Following P H Matthews (*Morphology*, CUP 1979), we will refer to orthographic and phonological words as 'word-forms'. These are words viewed as combinations of letters or combinations of sounds, respectively. In languages that are well-established in the written medium, the question of what constitutes an orthographic word-form poses few problems: the convention of writing 'words' with spaces either side provides the answer, except in the case of emergent compounds. For example, is *bird bath* spelt thus as two orthographic word-forms, or hyphenated *bird-bath*, or together *birdbath*, the last two counting each as one word-form. Decisions of this

47

nature at the orthographic level are generally dependent on prior lexical or phonological decisions about word status.

Phonologically, the question of what is a word is considerably more fraught. In some languages, there are clear phonological indicators of word boundaries. In languages with a fixed stress, where the main (or primary) stress falls on the same syllable in every word, a clear word pattern emerges. Another such indicator, which may combine with that of fixed stress, is the syllable structure in a language. Some languages have a very simple syllable structure, which does not allow combinations of consonants within a syllable; in those which do allow consonant clusters, there are specifiable constraints on combinations. For example, in the sequence /bɔldtri/ "bald tree" in English, the boundary would have to be established between /d/ and /t/, because the only permissible consonant clusters are /ld/ syllable-finally and /tr/ syllable-initially. A few languages exhibit a further phonological feature that contributes to the establishing of phonological word-forms, a feature termed 'vowel harmony'. This feature, found for example in Turkish (see Exercise 17), means that within a given word all the vowels will be of a given type (eg back rounded), so that a new syllable with a vowel not of this type will indicate the beginning of a new word.

In spite of these kinds of phonological indicators, it is extremely difficult in some languages to establish word forms phonologically. French is a notorious example, with stress distributed at utterance rather than word level and with extensive contraction of 'grammatical' words. Consider the following sequence: /ʒənleʒamɛvy/ "je ne l'ai jamais vu" ('I have never seen him/her'), where it is difficult to apply any of the phonological criteria we have discussed.

Lexemes

The term that has been coined to refer to 'words' from the point of view of the dictionary (or lexicon) is 'lexeme', on the pattern of 'phoneme' and 'morpheme'. 'Words' in this sense correspond to the headwords of dictionary entries. So far we have assumed that a lexeme comprises a single word-form, but this is by no means always the case. One problematical area is that of compound words (cf Chapter 7). Many compounds are identifiable as a single word-form because they adopt phonological characteristics of ordinary words, eg a single primary stress in English or German: *dríftwood*, *Dámpfschifffahrt* 'stéamboat joúrney'. But other root + or combinations, that one would want to recognise as compounds semantically root grammatically, do not adopt these phonological characteristics, eg *sélf-séeker*, whose compound status is recognised orthographically by the hyphen. Other compounds, whose single-word status is confirmed phonologically are, nevertheless, written as two word-forms, eg *cáttle grid*, *cárrier pigeon*. Another group of lexemes in English that has single-word status phonologically but not orthographically are the prepositional and phrasal verbs, eg *look after*, *look up* (ie 'visit'), *look up to*—to which we shall return later.

Leaving compounds aside, there are other combinations of word-forms that constitute a single item lexically: these are 'fixed phrases', such as metaphors or idioms, eg *on the straight and narrow*, *hammer and tongs*, *get the wrong end of the stick*. Characteristic of such expressions, which occur as items in many dictionaries and are thus to be treated as single lexemes, is that their meaning cannot be read off from the meaning of their constituents and that they have become institutionalised as 'fixed phrases' with idiosyncratic meanings. There is, however, in English at least, no clear boundary between sequences of words, whose meaning derives from the amalgamation of the meaning of each constituent word, and those fixed phrases whose meaning is not derivable in this way. For example, there are sequences of words that regularly occur together (collocations), of which one member only does not have its usual meaning, eg "a happy chance". *Happy* is normally predicated of people, and here the meaning is slightly different from its normal usage: do we then count "happy chance" as one lexeme or two? For any particular language there may well not be any clear-cut answers; lexicographers of English have varied in their judgements of what are to be counted as lexemes in the language. Clearly, though, there may be no direct one-to-one correspondence between lexeme and word-form in a language.

Words

We reserve the term 'word' for the grammatical level of analysis. Words are units of grammar, whose structure is described in terms of morphemes, and which enter into the structure of units at higher levels of grammatical patterning, eg phrases and clauses. The different forms of lexemes (eg *sing*, *sings*, *singing*, *sang*, *sung* as forms of SING) thus constitute separate words grammatically. Equally, homonyms like *skins* (plural of noun *skin*) and *skins* (3rd person singular present tense of verb *to skin*) are different grammatical words. So are the plural, the possessive, and the plural possessive, all represented by the pronunciation /gɛlz/ (but spelt *girls*, *girl's*, *girls'* respectively).

One classic definition of the 'word' regards it as "the minimal free form", ie the smallest unit that may occur on its own, eg as a one-word response to a question. Clearly, under this definition an inflectional morpheme would be excluded from word status, since it may only occur bound to a root morpheme or stem. However, such a definition also calls into question the status of many so-called 'grammatical' or 'form'-words, for example the articles (*a* and *the* in English). It would be unusual to hear *the* as a one-word response, except as a reply to a request for clarification ("Did you say *a* tiger or *the* tiger?"—"The"); but such replies may also comprise bound morphemes ("Did you say *dis*belief or *un*belief?"—"Dis").

The status of *the* as a word, as of 'form'-words generally, depends not on their ability to function as minimal responses, but on their detachability from other words and their relative freedom of occurrence. For example, *the* may occur directly before nouns ("the tiger"), before adjectives ("the ferocious tiger"), before quantifiers and numerals ("the many/seven ferocious tigers"), etc. If *the* is not to be regarded as free, and thus grammatically a word, it would be necessary to find some other class of word or morpheme to which it would be affixed: from our examples it is clear that this is not the case. An alternative solution would be to say that *the* is neither a word nor a bound morpheme, but has some indeterminate status, eg as a 'particle'—of which more below.

We consider first of all whether the 'word' or the 'morpheme' is to be considered the smallest unit of grammar. The traditional division of grammar into morphology and syntax regards the word as pivotal in both: in morphology it is the unit whose structure is described in terms of morphemes; and in syntax it is the smallest unit in the analysis of sentences. However, different types of language will lead to alternative evaluations of the relative status of word and morpheme. In an 'isolating' language like Vietnamese, where there are no inflectional or derivational affixes, it may be questionable whether a distinction between word and morpheme is strictly necessary. In an 'agglutinating' language like Turkish, where each morph realises only one morpheme, so that every word can be segmented into units, each of which has a single 'meaning', it would seem sensible not to insist on a division between morphology and syntax, but to regard the morpheme as the smallest unit in the syntactic hierarchy. In a 'synthetic' language like Latin, however, where a segment of a word (a morph) may realise a number of 'meanings' (eg the -*a* of *puella* 'girl' realises 'nominative' case, 'singular' number, 'feminine' gender), the distinction between morphology (as the description of the grammar of the word) and syntax (the description of the grammar of the sentence) is essential. We have described the three classic types of language: few languages conform exclusively in their structure to one only of these types. Linguistic analysts, therefore, need to make judgements on the relative status of word and morpheme in the description of a particular language on the basis of the nature of that individual language.

Consider now the following data (SIL 1980: K1) from Kaiwa (Brazil). Word boundaries are not marked!

1.	iwɨ'tuma	'The wind is already blowing (*lit.* 'It's winding')
2.	iwɨ'tupo'rā	'lovely wind'
3.	ipo'rāiwɨ'tu	'The wind is lovely'
4.	ipɨ'tāha'gwe	'Its feathers are red'
5.	ha'gwepi'tāpo'rā	'Its feathers are a beautiful red'
6.	iho'viha'gwe	'Its feathers are green'
7.	ha'gweho'vipo'râ	'Its feathers are a beautiful green'
8.	ha'gwema	'It already has feathers' (*lit.* 'It's feathering')
9.	ipo'rāha'gwe	'Its feathers are beautiful'

In this data it is clear that some items occur in the same position with respect to other (kinds of) items, while for others their relative position is variable. In particular: -*ma*, which is a 'verbaliser' (deriving a verb from a noun), and *i*-, also a 'verbaliser' (but deriving a verb from an adjective), must be regarded as bound morphemes. The other items, however, which we establish as items on the basis of their non-interruptibility, must be regarded as words, since they are mobile items: *ha'gwe* 'feathers', *iwɨ'tu* 'wind'; *ho'vi* 'green', *pi'tā* 'red', *po'rā* 'lovely/beautiful'.

Particles

We now take up the question of items which are clearly not morphemes, because of their relative freedom of occurrence, but which do not seem to attain to full word status. We earlier cited the question of *the* in English. A further example from English would be the so-called 'adverb particles', which combine with lexical verbs to form 'phrasal verbs', eg *look up* (= 'visit'), *slow down, give in, knock out, bring on* (= 'induce'), *take off* (= 'imitate'). These are regarded as single lexemes (eg in the *Longman Dictionary of Contemporary English*), but they are not compounds, because the adverb particle may be separated from the lexical verb (eg "the boxer knocked him out"), neither is the adverb particle an affix morpheme, for the same reason. But it is not a free word, since it is clearly part of the verb lexeme; and like the article, an adverb particle may not normally be the locus of intonational prominence in speech.

Another interesting case in English is that of the items *more* and *most*, which along with the suffixes *-er* and *-est* are 'allomorphs' of the 'comparative' and 'superlative' morphemes respectively. They are not affix morph(eme)s, however, since they may occur before words other than adjectives, eg nouns (cf "more difficult", "more money"; "most decisive", "most respect"). Should we, then, perhaps regard them as particles, since they are like affix morph(eme)s in respect of the inflections of the adjective, but like words in their general behaviour in the sentence?

In German, a set of word-forms called 'modal particles' occurs, including *doch, ja, wohl, (ein)mal*. They never receive any intonational prominence, have a generally 'emphatic' function, and are frequently not translatable (into English, at least!). For example: "Sie wissen *doch*, wie das so ist" ('You know how it is, don't you?'), "Das kann *wohl mal* vorkommen" ('That might well happen').

If we define particles as items that do not have bound morpheme status, but are not clearly words because they are generally unable to function as minimal responses, we ought probably to include prepositions and conjunctions within the category of particle. Prepositions, after all, are often functionally equivalent to inflectional affixes of synthetic languages, cf Latin *urbe* 'from the city', Old High German *swertu* 'with a sword'.

Clitics

Particles are items that have a marginal status as words. Clitics are items that have a marginal status as morphemes. That is to say, they clearly form part of another word, eg on phonological grounds, but they are moveable and do not regularly form part of one particular class of words. A candidate for the status of clitic in English is the 'possessive' suffix, which we generally regard as being an inflectional suffix of the noun. It does not, however, always occur on the noun: if the noun is postmodified (see Chapter 13), the 'possessive' clitic is attached to the last item in the noun phrase; cf "the president*'s* proposals", "the president of the United States of America*'s* proposals", "the president who addressed the nation yesterday*'s* proposals". The last of these examples is perhaps less likely to occur; in such cases the alternative formulation with *of* is probably preferred ("the proposals of the president, who addressed the nation yesterday").

Also a candidate for clitic status is the Latin item *-que* 'and', which only occurs as part of another word, but which may be affixed to almost any word, eg "pueri puellaeque" 'boys and girls', "*vir mulierque*" 'a man and a woman'.

Consider now the following data (SIL 1980: K11) from Choctaw (USA):

1. alatik-mat talowa   'the girl sings'
   girl   sings
2. alatik osi-mat talowa   'the little girl sings'
   girl   little   sings
3. alatik osi   taθapi-mat talowa   'the four little girls sing'
   girl   little four   sing
4. hatak-mat abilini-ma pilatok   'the man threw the chair'
   man   chair   threw
5. hatak-mat abilini chite-ma pilatok   'the man threw the big chair'
   man   chair big   threw
6. hatak-mat abilini-ma ayimpa-pito pilatok
   man   chair   table-on   threw

                                                  'the man threw the chair on the table'

7. hatak-mat abilini-ma alatik osi-pito pilatok
   man   chair   girl   little-to threw

                                                  'the man threw the chair at the little
                                                  girl'

Here the items *-mat*, *-ma* and *-pito* are to be regarded as clitics; they are affixed to stems, but not always to the same stem. The item *-mat* is a subject-marker and it occurs on the last item of the noun phrase functioning as subject, whether that is a noun (No 1), an adjective (No 2), or a numeral (No 3). The item *-ma* is an object marker and occurs similarly on a noun (No 4), or an adjective (No 5). The item *-pito* is a postposition, occurring on the last item of the noun phrase governed by it, a noun (No 6) or an adjective (No 7).

We must conclude, therefore, that the descriptive status of words, morphemes and any other intermediate unit (particles and clitics) must depend on the nature of the individual language and on the considered judgement of the linguistic analyst describing that language.

Exercise 20

Consider which items in the following Tlingit (Alaska) data (SIL 1980: K9) might be regarded as particles or clitics.

1. ax hidee-t   oowagut   'He went to (and arrived at) my house'
   my house-poss-to he-went
2. ax hidee   tlen-t oowagut   'He went to my big house'
   my house-poss big-to he went
3. ax hidee-dei   woogoot   'He went to (towards) my house'
   my house-poss-to he-went
4. ax hidee   tlen-dei woogoot   'He went to my big house'
   my house-poss big-to   he-went
5. doo aat-gaa woogoot   'He went for (to fetch) his aunt'
   his aunt-for he-went
6. doo aat   has-gaa woogoot   'He went to fetch his aunts'
   his aunt pl.-for he-went

7. ax aat nak   ax hide-dei woogoot   'He went to my house without my aunt'
   my aunt without my house-to he-went

8. doo aat has nak   woogoot   'He went without his aunts'
   his aunt pl. without he-went

9. tleil doo aat   teen woogoot   'He didn't go with his aunt'
   neg. his aunt with he-went

10. doo aat   has teen woo.aat   'He went with his aunts'
    his aunt pl. with he-went

10. Sentences (1)

Nouns and verbs

Sentences may be viewed essentially as the combinations of nouns and verbs. More precisely, a sentence may be viewed as the combination of a verb with one or more nouns. We mentioned earlier that nouns refer to the 'things' of our experience (persons, objects, ideas, feelings, etc), and that verbs refer to 'events' (including actions, processes and states). Sentences, then, are concerned with the myriad ways in which the 'things' of experience are involved in the 'events' of experience, or rather with the myriad ways in which we are able to talk about them.

Consider the following sentences of English:

1. Horses eat hay.
2. The committee has awarded the novelist first prize.
3. The heckler argued with the speaker about his ideas.
4. The children played in the garden after tea.

The first of these sentences contains just one verb and two nouns: the verb refers to an 'action', and the nouns to the 'things' involved in the action. In the second sentence, the structure still essentially comprises a verb and nouns (viz *award*, *committee*, *novelist*, *prize*): the additional words are dependent on or modify these main items. Similarly in the third sentence, where the verb and nouns are *argue*, *heckler*, *speaker*, *ideas*; except that here, besides 'modifying' words like *the* and *his*, there are also 'relational' words (prepositions) like *with* and *about*. The fourth sentence (in which the verb and nouns are *play*, *children*, *garden*, *tea*) also has prepositions (*in*, *after*) in addition to modifiers, but here the prepositions have a spatial and temporal reference respectively, and are substitutable. The function of the prepositions in No 4 is thus different from that of the prepositions in No 3: you can only argue *with* somebody *about* something; but you can play *in*, *on*, *outside*, etc somewhere, *after*, *before*, *at*, etc, some point in time. But the basic point remains: sentences are essentially structures comprising a verb and a number of nouns.

The verb is central

A useful way of approaching the analysis of sentence structure is to regard the verb as the central element which determines how many (and which kind of) nouns may be present in a sentence, including any non-substitutable relational items (eg prepositions and case inflections). This function of the verb as the determining element in a sentence derives from a 'dependency' view of sentence structure (see Chapter 22). Which other elements a verb determines is attributable to the 'meaning' of the verb. For example, we implied earlier that the verb *argue* determines the presence of three nouns: *someone* argue with *someone* about *something*. In fact, our English specification allows us to indicate additionally that two of the nouns refer to persons and one to a non-person. Clearly, this kind of statement has a good measure of generality, since other kinds of sentence structure occur with *argue* that make some refinements of this statement necessary; eg "The boys are arguing", "He is arguing with his sister", "They are arguing about the rules of the game". Two further points need to be noticed about *argue*: firstly, it may be used to refer generally to the action, when only the participants in the argument are mentioned, but not the 'something' argued about; secondly, the participants in the argument may be collected together as one (plural) noun (*the boys*, *they*), with or without mention of the 'something' argued about.

Consider another example: *buy*. This verb could be said to determine the following nouns: *someone* buy *something* from *someone/somewhere* for *some amount*, eg "Bill bought the radio from the corner shop for £10". We might add: at *some time*, eg "the day before yesterday"; though we might regard this as not being strictly determined by the verb *buy*, since almost any event may be specified for point of time. A refinement of this general statement for *buy* would have to indicate that not all of the nouns need to be specified, ie that the someone/somewhere from which the thing is bought and the amount for which it is bought may be omitted (eg "Jack has bought a new car", "Bill bought a radio for £10", "Harry buys his newspapers from the corner shop").

English does not have case marking for sentence elements. We will now consider a couple of examples from German, which does mark case (though as we have seen—Chapter 3—not in the noun itself). Our first example is *geben* 'give', which determines as follows: *someone* (nominative case) geben *someone* (dative case) *something* (accusative case), eg "Der Mann hat seiner Frau einen Diamanten gegeben" 'The man gave his wife a diamond'. Our second example from German is *anklagen* 'accuse', which determines as follows (*wegen* is a preposition often translated by 'because of' in English): *someone* (nominative case) anklagen *someone* (accusative case) wegen *something* (genitive case), eg "Die Polizei hat den Gefangenen wegen des Diebstahls angeklagt" 'The police accused the prisoner of theft'.

Exercise 21

Make 'determining' statements for the following English verbs, adding any 'refining' details you think necessary:

1. write
2. win
3. spend
4. wait
5. invite
6. clean
7. fight
8. report

Sentence types

From the limited number of examples that we have looked at so far in this chapter, it has probably not been apparent that for any language a limited number of patterns of sentence structure occurs. That is to say, it is possible to make generalisations about the types of sentence patterns that occur in a language, many of which are applicable across languages.

Traditionally, a distinction has been made between 'transitive' and 'intransitive' sentences. Intransitive sentences have only one noun directly involved in the event: the 'doer' of an action, or the 'undergoer' of a process; eg "The children are laughing", "The tree is falling". In transitive sentences, more than one noun is directly involved in the event, though usually not more than three. The second noun usually refers to the 'undergoer' in an action, eg "The goalkeeper caught the ball". The third noun, in what is sometimes called a 'ditransitive' sentence, usually refers to the 'recipient' or 'beneficiary' involved in the action, eg "The shopkeeper sent the customer a bill". In German, and other languages with case systems, these different nouns are identifiable by their case marking: in German, the first noun (ie the one occurring alone in intransitive sentences, and the 'doer' in transitive ones) is in the nominative case, the second noun is in the accusative case, and the third noun is in the dative case.

Two further sentence types commonly found are 'stative' and 'equative' sentences, both of which are characterised by the presence of the verb *be* in English (though this is not the only verb which may occur), eg

Stative:	"The leaves are brown".
Equative:	"Harry is the ship's doctor".

In the case of stative sentences, the second (non-verbal) element is often—as in our example—an adjective rather than a noun; though we could equally well say "The leaves are a brown colour", where the second element is now a noun (*colour*), modified by an adjective (*brown*). In stative sentences the adjective or second noun describes (the state of) the first noun. In equative sentences, as the term suggests, there is an equational relationship between the two nouns; their order is often reversible, eg we could have said for our example "The ship's doctor is Harry", though this would have a different contextual meaning. In languages that have case inflections (eg Latin, German), the second element is often in the same case as the first noun (eg nominative case), cf German "Dieser Mann ist der Schiffsarzt" 'This man is the ship's doctor'.

Our list of sentence types is by no means exhaustive. Each language must be considered on its merits, on the basis of the possible generalisations from occurring sentence patterns. Consider now the following data from Kolami (India):

1. amd mangten   'he slept'
   he slept
2. add ellang seddin   'she went to the house'
   she house went
3. amd aambal tinden   'he ate rice'
   he rice   ate
4. amd anung pustok siyten   'he gave me a book'
   he me   book gave
5. ramak poḍam anḍan   'Ram is tall'
   Ram tall   is

Here we can clearly recognise an intransitive sentence (No 1), with just one noun and an action verb; a transitive sentence (No 3), with two nouns and an action verb; and a ditransitive sentence (No 4), with three nouns. No 5 falls into the stative (or 'descriptive') type, with a noun and an adjective describing the noun. No 2 is somewhat of a problem, since it looks like a transitive sentence, with two nouns; but the action verb *go* does not involve the second noun (*ellang* 'house') in the same way that *tinden* 'ate' involves *aambal* 'rice', ie the house does not have something done to it. Rather, the house is the place or the location, towards which the action is directed. Such sentence types, with a location as the second noun but structured like a transitive sentence, are often called 'semi-transitive' sentences; they occur typically in North-Indian languages.

Exercise 22

Identify the sentence types in the following Engenni (Nigeria) data (SIL 1980: E7):

1. edei nɛ adidɛ   'The man is a rich man'
    man the rich-man
2. Ade misɛ n'eki   'Ade slept in the market'
        slept in-market
3. Ade doriya   'Ade is tall'
            is-tall
4. edei nɛ mɔni ozhi avu n'ukwo   'The man saw a thief at the farm'
    man the saw   thief one at-farm
5. Ade do   eseni   'Ade stole a fish'
        stole fish
6. eseni kuya   'Fish is scarce'
    fish   is-scarce
7. edei nɛ fina n'ɔkɔ   'The man entered the canoe'
    man the enter in-canoe
8. adidɛ   nɛ wu   'The rich man died'
    rich-man the died
9. edei dori nɛ Ade   'The tall man is Ade'
    man tall the

Sentences without verbs

In the previous exercise, two of the examples were sentences without a verb (Nos 1 and 9), which would seem to contradict our earlier statement that a sentence was constituted by a verb and one or more nouns. In fact, that statement does not have general validity because of one other kind of sentence: one that contains only a verb, eg Latin "Pluit" 'It is raining'. But the more interesting cases of the statement not being valid are those where there is no verb. In the Engenni data (Exercise 22), the sentences without verbs are equative sentences. And we find that it is not unusual for equative and stative/descriptive sentences to be verbless (where in English the verb *be* would be used).

Consider the following examples from Western Desert (Australia):

1. wati mirpanpa   'The man is angry'
    man angry
2. wati ngalyayala   'The man is a doctor'
            doctor

Similarly in Hixkaryana (Brazil) for equative sentences, eg

1. Hoňko woto   'The game is/was wild pig'
   wild-pig game
2. Towankařhemɨ anaro komo   'Others were courageous'
   courageous-one other group

And in Tlingit (Alaska) there is a locative sentence that is verbless, eg

1. ee   xòonee nèilu   'Your friend is at home'
   your friend   inside-LM
2. aatlèin dáanaa doo jèewu   'He has lots of money'
   lots   money his hand-LM

(LM = locative marker, ie an inflection signalling location).

Exercise 23

Identify the sentence types of the examples in the following data (SIL 1980: E8) based on Pocomchi (Guatemala):

1. huan ʃokik   pan ripat   'John entered his house'
   John entered in   his-house
2. re huan ʃilwatʃ   rasbes   'John recognised his older brother'
              recognised older-brother
3. re ribahil   maria huan   'John is Mary's husband'
   her-husband Mary John
4. riʃq'un   na rik'uʃum tulul   'Her daughter will eat bananas'
   her-daughter will eat   bananas
5. re tulul   ʃirix   pat   'The bananas are behind the house'
   the bananas behind house
6. re   kinaq' wiki   'The beans are there'
        beans   there
7. re   maria re riʃq'un   'Her daughter is Mary'
        Mary   her-daughter
8. re be   inox pan tinamit   'The road goes into town'
      road goes in   town
9. ripat   ʃirix   k'aybal   'Her house is behind the market'
   her-house behind market
10. maria na ri'ayem tulul   pan tinamit 'Mary will sell bananas in town'
    Mary will sell   bananas in   town

11. Sentences (2)

In the previous chapter we characterised sentences as combinations of a verb and one or more nouns, which may in turn have associated with them modifiers (eg adjectives) and be linked to the verb by a relational device (preposition or case inflection). Sentences were distinguished by type according to the number of nouns determined by the verb and their relationships to the verb and in some cases to each other. We will now identify and give labels to the functions that the verb and the nouns perform in the structure of sentences.

Functions

The function performed by the verb in a sentence we refer to as the 'Predicator' function: the verb 'predicates' an action, process or state of a noun or nouns. The element that we referred to as the 'first noun' in the previous chapter performs the 'Subject' function in a sentence: it is the agent of an action Predicator, the under-goer of a process, the 'thing' of which a location or state is predicated. There is often person and number agreement (see Chapter 16) between the noun functioning as Subject and the verb functioning as Predicator. Consider the present tense paradigm of the verb *travailler* 'work' in French: je travaille, tu travailles, il/elle travaille, noun travaillons, vous travaillez, ils/elles travaillent. That is to say, "tu travailles" is analysed as 'Subject:noun—Predicator:verb', with the categories of '2nd person'/'singular number' of the Subject *tu* marked in the Predicator *travailles* by means of the *-es* suffix—working here from the written rather than the spoken forms.

The 'second noun' in a sentence may perform a number of functions, depending on the sentence type in which it occurs. In a transitive sentence the second noun performs the function of 'Object' in the sentence: it represents the undergoer of the action, the 'object' towards which the action is directed, eg *the camp-fire* in "The boy-scout lit the camp-fire". The second noun in a stative or equative sentence has the syntactic function of 'Complement', eg in sentences like "The journey was *a frightening experience*", "Harry is *the carpenter*". The Complement refers back to and elaborates or describes the Subject of the sentence. As we have seen, in stative sentences the Complement function may be performed by an adjective rather than a noun, eg "The journey was *frightening*". The second noun in sentences of the locative or temporal type functions as an 'Adjunct', representing additional, circumstantial information about a Subject or a predicated action or event, as in "The children are *in the garden*", "Our guests departed *the day before yesterday*". Second nouns, then, may function syntactically as Object, Complement or Adjunct, according to the sentence type, or ultimately according to the meaning of the verb functioning as Predicator.

We turn now to the syntactic functions of a possible third noun in a sentence. In the previous chapter we mentioned one sentence type that contained a third noun: the ditransitive type, eg "We sent all our friends a postcard"/"We sent a postcard to all our friends", where (*to*) *all our friends* is considered the third noun. We noticed that the third noun usually has the semantic function of 'recipient' or 'beneficiary'. Syntactically, the third noun in ditransitive sentences functions as Object; that is to say, in ditransitive sentences there are two nouns functioning as Object. A distinction is sometimes drawn between the 'Direct Object' (the second noun, 'directly' involved in the action) and the 'Indirect Object' (the third noun, only 'indirectly' involved).

There are two further not uncommon sentence types that contain a third noun. The first can be illustrated from English by the following sentence: "We thought Harry's death a terrible tragedy". Here *we* is analysed as Subject, *thought* as Predicator, *Harry's death* as Object, and *a terrible tragedy* as Complement. The Complement now refers back to and elaborates the Object (rather than the Subject as in stative sentences). This sentence type could perhaps be called a 'transitive/stative' type. The second further type with a third noun can be illustrated from English by: "The carpenter keeps his tools in a leather bag". Here *the carpenter* is analysed as Subject, *keeps* as Predicator, *his tools* as Object, and *in a leather bag* as Adjunct. The Adjunct in this sentence type gives information on the location of the Object (rather than of the Subject as in the locative type). This type could perhaps be called a 'transitive/locative' sentence type. Both sentence types just discussed are sometimes referred to as 'complex-transitive'.

Identifying syntactic functions

We have so far attempted to characterise syntactic functions by alluding to their role in the economy of particular sentence types. Another identification procedure is to examine the kinds of questions that relate to each of the functions. The Subject of a sentence is elicited by questions like: "*Who/What* is/did something?", "*What* happened?" The Object of a sentence is elicited by: "*What/Who(m)* did someone do?" or "*To/For Who(m)* did someone do something?" (Indirect Object). The Adjunct of a sentence is elicited by: "*Where/When/How/Why* did someone do something?" or ". . . did something happen?" or ". . . is something?". The Complement of a sentence is elicited by: "*What* is someone/something?"

This procedure may be combined with one that starts with the verb functioning as Predicator and asks what additional elements are determined by that particular verb (cf Chapter 10). For example, the verb *send* could be said to determine *someone* who sends ("*Who* sends?"), *something* that is sent ("*What* did someone send?"), and *someone* to whom it is sent ("*To whom* did someone send something?") or *somewhere* it is sent ("*Where* did someone send something?"). That is, *send* enters either a ditransitive sentence type (containing two Objects) or a transitive/locative sentence type (containing Object and Adjunct).

Functions and sentence types

It is now possible to look again at sentence types and to describe them in terms of the syntactic functional slots that each of them opens up. The intransitive sentence type, for example, opens up a Subject and a Predicator slot only, the ditransitive type a Subject, a Predicator and two Object slots. We can summarise the structure of sentence types that we have discussed in the following table (where S is Subject, P is Predicator, O is Object, C is Complement, A is Adjunct):

Intransitive	S P
Stative or Equative	S P C
Locative or Temporal	S P A
Transitive	S P O
Ditransitive	S P O O
Transitive/Stative	S P O C
Transitive/Locative	S P O A

It should be noted that the list is not complete, in the sense that many languages have more, fewer, or different sentence types than these. Also, the order of the elements in the sentence types above corresponds to the 'neutral' order for English, and other languages that place Subject before Predicator and Objects or Complement after the Predicator. Other languages have a different 'neutral' or 'basic' order; eg Western Desert (Australia) has SOP order: "watilu maku kultunu" (*lit.* 'man kangaroo speared').

Exercise 24

Identify for the following English sentences which sentence type is represented, and indicate which words belong to each functional position; eg "Bill (S) sent (P) his wife (O) a message (O)"—ditransitive.

1. The shipyard is building a new oil-tanker.
2. Harry is sitting in the garden.
3. The children will put their muddy boots on the kitchen floor.
4. Susan is a first-class journalist.
5. Last night's storm blew over the tree in the corner.
6. The committee has appointed Edward as its secretary.
7. Our parking time expired five minutes ago.
8. Harry was telling us a funny story.
9. The branch is breaking.
10. My coat is the brown one.

Obligatory and optional elements

We have discussed the structure so far in terms of a verb and a number of nouns, functioning in positions opened up according to sentence type, or alternatively, determined by the 'meaning' of the verb. The implication has been that a verb 'requires' a specific number of nouns in order for the sentence to be 'grammatical' or 'complete', or to 'make sense'. We have noted, eg in the case of English *send*, that a verb may function as Predicator in more than one sentence type (ditransitive and transitive/locative for *send*). But all the functional positions determined by the verb or implied by the sentence type have been filled. That is to say, we have been dealing so far only with 'obligatory' elements of sentences.

There are two senses in which an element of sentence structure may be regarded as 'optional' rather than 'obligatory'. First of all, it is possible to add elements to sentences that are not directly required by the verb. Consider: "The agent gave me the parcel yesterday in the park". *Give* is a ditransitive verb; it requires a Subject (*the agent*) and two Objects (*me, the parcel*). The sentence would be grammatical or complete with just these slots filled: *yesterday* and *in the park* are thus gratuitous elements that have been added to the basic sentence type. Note that they are both functioning as Adjunct, as a temporal and a locative Adjunct respectively. It is possible to specify time and place for almost any event, but it is arguable that few verbs actually require them to be specified. Optional Adjuncts—of time, place, manner, reason, purpose, etc—may be freely added to almost any sentence, depending on the contraints of context.

The second sense in which it is possible to speak of an 'optional' element in sentence structure entails the omission of an element that is regarded as being required by the verb. Consider the verb *write* in English. Arguably this verb enters a ditransitive sentence type, ie 'someone *write* something *to/for* someone' (eg "Harry is writing a letter to his aunt", "Harry is writing a report for the director"). But it is possible to omit either or both of the Objects, eg "Harry is writing" (in answer to the question "What's Harry doing?"), "Harry is writing a letter", "Harry is writing to his aunt". In the case of a verb like *write* we must say either that *write* enters the intransitive and transitive sentence types as well as the ditransitive, or that *write* is basically ditransitive but that either or both Objects are in some sense 'optional'. Clearly, this is a different kind of optionality from the first kind; and it may be more appropriate to distinguish it by referring to it as 'deletability' rather than optionality. That is, the Objects of *write* are said to be 'deletable' according to the conditions of context; for it is usually the case that context determines or allows the deletability of otherwise obligatory elements of sentence structure. It is probably also the case that a semantically restricted Object is more likely to be deleted than one not so restricted; for example, Indirect Objects nearly always refer to persons and are thus probably more often deletable, and in the case of a verb like *write*, the Direct Object is more-or-less restricted to a set of nouns referring to written artefacts (cf also *read, sing, play*).

Functions and classes

We began our discussion of sentences by asserting that a sentence is essentially made up of a verb and some accompanying nouns. We have had to revise that assertion in the intervening pages, in order to account for verbless sentences and to allow for adjectives appearing instead of nouns. Having now introduced the functional slots of sentence structure, we need to bring the functions into relationship with the classes (or categories) of word (ie noun, verb, etc).

The Predicator functional slot is filled by a verb, along with any of its accompanying modifying elements (eg auxiliary verbs, negative particles), ie by what might be called a 'verb phrase'. The Subject slot is usually filled by a noun, along with its accompanying modifying elements (see Chapters 12 and 13), ie by a 'noun phrase', or by a pronoun or proper noun (name). Pronouns and proper nouns are not usually accompanied by any modifying elements, and in any case the possibilities are normally restricted. For example, in English a pronoun may be postmodified by a relative clause (see Chapter 13): "he who hesitates". But compare the equivalents of this in French and German: "celui qui hésite" 'the one who hesitates', ie not using the pronoun *il* 'he'; "wer zögert" 'who hesitates', ie not using the pronoun *er* 'he'.

The Object slot is also usually filled by a noun phrase or pronoun or proper noun. It may additionally be accompanied by a preposition or postposition, eg "I gave it *to* John", French "Je l'ai donné *à* Jean"; Hindi "us *se* yah saval puchie", literally 'him-to this question ask' (ie "Ask him this question"). The Complement slot is usually filled either by a noun phrase or by an adjective and any accompanying modifiers it might have (see Chapter 14), ie by an 'adjective phrase'. These may also be accompanied by a preposition or postposition, eg "I regard him *as* a friend". Finally, the Adjunct slot may be filled by a number of categories: a noun phrase, a noun phrase accompanied by a preposition or postposition, or an adverb; eg Hindi "vah apne ghar laut gaya" 'he his home back went' (ie "he returned to his home"), "budhvar ko ao" 'Wednesday on come' (ie "Come on Wednesday"), "vah accha gati hai" 'she well singing is' (ie "she sings well").

It is thus possible to describe the structure of a sentence by identifying both the functional slots and the categories of word or phrase that fill them. For example:

"The keeper (S: Noun Phrase) is giving (P: Verb Phrase) the lions (Oi: Noun Phrase) their meat (Od: Noun Phrase)".
"Our friends (S: NP) live (P: VP) in Brussels (A: Prepositional Phrase)".
"This room (S: NP) feels (P: VP) very cold (C: Adjective Phrase)".

Exercise 25

For the following data (SIL 1980: E13) from Tlingit (Alaska), make an analysis of each sentence identifying functional slots and categories of phrase that fill them, and indicate which sentence type each belongs to.

1. xóots   saxwaa.áx   dzeeyáak   'I heard a brown bear earlier on'
   brown-bear voice-I-heard earlier-on
2. Juneau-dé kukgwaatèen   'He's going to Juneau on a trip'
              he-will-take-a-trip
3. kúnax kusi.áat'   'It's really cold'
   really it-is-cold
4. tlax   a yáanax   ee wdixwétl   'You're too tired'
   too-much it face-beyond you is-tired
5. ee xòonee   'It's your friend'
   your friend
6. aatlèin dáanaa doo jèewoo   'He has lots of money'
   lots   money his hand-locative marker

12. Expanding the noun (1)

Noun phrase

We referred in the previous chapter to the possibility of a noun, functioning at a particular position in sentence structure, being accompanied by one or more modifying elements. And we termed this combination a 'noun phrase'. Some descriptive linguists would recognise a phrase level of syntactic structure intermediate between word and sentence. That is, the structure of a sentence is described in terms of its constituent phrases, and these phrases in turn are described in terms of their constituent words. So the general definition of a 'phrase' becomes: "a unit consisting of one or more words". In such a descriptive framework each unit is described in terms of the units at the level immediately below.

In this book we have taken the view so far that sentences are considered to be combinations of words, which may in turn be accompanied by modifying items. That is to say, we are regarding 'sentence' and 'word' as the primitive terms in our syntactic description. And, as the titles of this chapter and the next two imply, we are regarding phrases as expansions of particular classes of words.

The class of nouns is the one, probably in all languages, that may be subject to the most and to the most varied expansion by modifying elements. In this chapter we consider the expansion of nouns by means of members of other word classes, and in the next chapter we look at modifiers that are themselves syntactic structures.

Closed class modifiers

Towards the end of Chapter 2 we identified a number of word classes that we termed 'closed' rather than 'open', because their membership is restricted in number, changes only very slowly over time, and can easily be listed exhaustively. Some of these classes function in the expansion of nouns, especially the class of Determiners.

The membership of the Determiner class varies from language to language, and it includes a number of quite diverse subsets of items, all of which, however, contribute to 'determining' the contextual status of a noun. First of all, a distinction is often made in the Determiner class between 'Identifiers' and 'Quantifiers'. As the latter label implies, these items have the function of specifying 'how many' or 'how much' of a particular noun is being referred to. Such a specification may either involve an actual number (*"five* coaches", "the *third* coach") or be an expression of indefinite quantity (*"several* coaches", *"some* cheese"). Clearly, there is a relation of compatibility here between quantifiers and the subclasses of 'mass' and 'countable' nouns. For example, *some* is compatible with the singular of mass nouns ("some cheese"), but with the plural of countable nouns ("some coaches"); and numerals are compatible with countable nouns only, unless they precede a specific expression of quantity ("five *pounds* of cheese", "twelve *litres* of petrol"). Compare German "einige Wagen" 'some coaches', "etwas Käse" 'some cheese'; and French "des wagons" 'some coaches', "du fromage" 'some cheese'.

The class of Identifiers includes, in English, the 'articles' (indefinite *a*, definite *the*), the demonstratives (*this*, *that*), the possessives (*my*, *your*, *his*, etc). In English these items are mutually exclusive, ie the occurrence of one excludes the possibility of the occurrence of the others in the same noun phrase; eg *"my the box" is not a possible noun phrase in English. Many languages (eg Latin) do not have items equivalent to the English articles: 'definiteness' is signalled in other ways. Neither do all languages show the same mutual occurrence restrictions as English.

Consider the following data (SIL 1980: B2) from Bekwarra (Nigeria):

1. ugam   '(the/a) mat'
2. ugam iyi   'my mat'
3. ugam itʃia   'three mats'
4. ugam abɨn   'this mat'
5. ugam iyi itʃia abɨn   'these three mats of mine'

Note that the modifiers of the noun come after it in Bekwarra, whereas the equivalent items in English come before the noun, except for *of mine* in the last example. This, however, is the English way of including a demonstrative and a possessive in the same noun phrase (cf *"my these mats"), a structure that is possible with the regular possessive identifier in Bekwarra. Note also, incidentally, that Bekwarra does not mark 'plural' number in either the noun or the demonstrative, as English does. A further descriptive point is the relative order of the modifiers in the noun phrase. From Item 5 we can describe the structure of the noun phrase in this Bekwarra data as: noun—possessive—numeral—demonstrative.

Exercise 26

Describe the structure of the noun phrase in the following Agatu (Nigeria) data (based on SIL 1980: B5):

1. ugwu oye   'one hen'
2. ugwu ɛhɔ   'five hens'
3. ugwu du   'all the hens'
4. ugwu ɛhɔ du lɔ   'all those five hens'

Open class modifiers

The most obvious and extensive class in this group is that of Adjectives, perhaps the set of words that most readily springs to mind in the context of noun modification. Adjectives referring to colour, size, shape, texture, provenance, etc, are widespread in the languages of the world. Very often they can function both as modifiers of nouns and in the predicate of a clause as Complement, eg "the *red* hat", "the hat is *red*". As we have noted already (Chapter 10), descriptive or stative sentences like this are frequently verbless. Within the noun phrase, some languages (like English) place the adjective before the noun, while others place it after, and yet others have adjectives in both positions. A language of this last kind is French, eg "le chapeau rouge" 'the hat red', "le bon enfant" 'the good child'; although noun-adjective is the more frequently occurring order, with the alternative limited to a relatively small set of common adjectives. English also has an adjective-following pattern, though not as a rule with nouns: indefinite pronouns, however, are normally followed by an adjective modifier, eg "somebody neutral", "anything unusual", "nothing alcoholic"; but cf "a little something", "an absolute nobody"—where the pronoun has more or less taken on the status of a noun.

When more than one adjective occurs as modifier of a noun, it may be the case that classes of adjective are ordered relative to each other. In English, for example, we would be more likely to say "the big red hat" than ?"the red big hat"—unless there were two 'big hats' and we wished to distinguish the red one from one of another colour, in which case *red* would carry contrastive stress. In English, then, adjectives referring to size normally precede those referring to colour. Compare French "le grand chapeau rouge", where the size adjective *grand* 'big' precedes the noun and the colour one, *rouge* 'red', follows it. It would appear that, in English, the more criterial the adjective is in distinguishing the noun, the closer it is put to it in the noun phrase, so that colour is normally considered more criterial than size.

Consider now the following data (based on SIL 1980: B7) from Mambila (Nigeria):

1. tèl   'elephant'
2. tèl búnu   'this elephant'
3. tèl achi   'your elephant'
4. tèl amòh búnu   'this elephant of mine'
5. tèl amòh dua   'my large elephant'
6. tèl dua yili   'a large black elephant'
7. tèl bonu fàl   'these two elephants'
8. tèl bonu dua yili fàl   'these two large black elephants'

From this data we can conclude that the structure of the noun phrase in Mambila may be expressed, at least partially, by the following formula: noun—possessive—demonstrative—adjective (size)—adjective (colour)—numeral. Here, too, the size adjective precedes the colour one, but is closer to the noun; though in Mambila the adjectives are separated from the noun by closed-class modifiers.

We have been talking of adjectives as if they were a universal class of words. This is by no means the case. Some languages have a class of modifying words that corresponds to the classes of adjective and adverb in English: compare the Apinaye (Brazil) data in Exercise 5 (Chapter 2). This is also the case, more or less, in German, where it can be said at least that there is a large overlap between the set of open-class modifiers of nouns and the set of items functioning as Adjunct in the predicate structure of sentences; cf "die schöne Sängerin" 'the beautiful singer', "sie singt sehr schön" 'she sings very beautifully'. What is widespread, if not indeed universal, is the occurrence of a set of open-class words that have as one of their functions the modification of nouns.

The other set of open-class modifiers of nouns is perhaps much less widespread: it is nouns themselves, functioning as modifiers of other nouns. For example, English "the felt hat", where the noun *felt* modifies *hat*. Arguably, this noun + noun combination (*felt hat*) could be considered as a compound (see Chapter 7), but it does not have the characteristic single primary stress on the first element (cf *fire-bucket*). Moreover, the modifying noun often co-varies with adjectives having similar reference (cf "the woollen hat") and the combination is not felt semantically to be a single unit. Possibly, however, there is considerable variation in degrees of cohesiveness between noun + noun compounds at one end of the scale and noun-modifier + noun combinations at the other.

Defining/non-defining

It is probably true to say that adjectives more often than not have a defining role; that is, they serve to assign the noun being modified to one subset of such nouns rather than another, or they distinguish the 'thing' being referred to by the modified noun from another possible 'thing' referred to by the same noun. For example, the adjective *red* in "the red hat" assigns this hat to the subset of hats distinguished by their being red; in "my red hat", *red* distinguishes this hat from hats of other colours that I might have. Such uses of adjectives are said to be 'defining'.

If, however, I have only one hat, then to refer to it as "my red hat" is to provide gratuitous and non-essential information. Indeed the adjective *red* would normally be understood as having a defining function in the phrase "my red hat"; and one would probably resort to other strategies if one intended *red* as non-defining, eg "I can't find my hat. It's red", where the indication of colour is intended as a clue to establishing its whereabouts. Arguably, in the expression "It's red", the adjective *red*, although no longer a modifier, has a defining function, assigning "my hat" to the subset of hats coloured red.

In the phrase "my lovely wife", however, the adjective *lovely* would normally be taken to have a non-defining function, assuming that it is spoken in a monogamous society! Similarly, the adjective *late* is non-defining in the phrase "his late father"; and the adjective *old* in the phrase "the old railway worker", where *old* is added merely as a characterising feature of the noun, not as a defining one. Note in this example, though, that the noun-modifier *railway* does have a defining function, assigning the noun *worker* to a particular subset of workers. The distinction between defining and non-defining will again be important in the discussion of clausal modifiers, especially relative clauses.

Definite vs indefinite

Many languages, including English, have overt means of marking a noun phrase as 'definite' or 'indefinite'. This is often done by means of a set of Determiners called 'Articles': *a* and *the* in English, 'indefinite' and 'definite' article respectively. The primary function of the articles is in the relationship between the sentences of a text or discourse. The indefinite article marks a noun as 'first mention' of a referent, while the definite article marks the noun as 'already introduced' into the discourse. For example, in the sentence "A Japanese team has climbed the mountain", the noun *mountain* is marked as a referent already under discussion, while *Japanese team* here receives its first mention.

In languages which do not have items equivalent to the articles of English (eg Russian, Bimoba), other means are used to indicate that a noun is to be interpreted as definite or indefinite. In Russian, for example, the positioning of a noun in the initial slot of a sentence marks it as definite. In Bimoba, special particles occur after nouns that have been mentioned before in the discourse. And in Lithuanian there is a special pronominal form of adjectives, used with nouns that have already been introduced into the discourse.

Another function that the definite article has (in English, for example), is to occur with nouns that are modified by a defining relative clause or prepositional phrase; eg "the woman that I saw you with yesterday", "the house with the red door". Note that both "a house with the red door" and "the house with a red door" sound odd in English, but not "a house with a red door".

Exercise 27

For the following data (SIL 1980: B1) based on Coatlán Mixe (Mexico) describe the structure of the noun phrase:

1. po:ʃ   tsu:tʃ   ʔiʃp   'The spider sees the horsefly'
   spider horsefly sees
2. he po:ʃ   tsu:tʃ   ka:jɨp   'That spider will eat the horsefly'
   that spider horsefly will-eat
3. tsu:k tʃi:t ʔiʃti   'The rat saw the cat'
   rat   cat saw
4. tʃi:t po:p tsu:k ʔiʃp   'The cat sees the white rat'
   cat white rat   sees
5. tʃi:t po:p tsu:k jahʔoʔokɨp   'The cat will kill the white rat'
   cat white rat   will-kill
6. po:p tʃi:t he po:p tsu:k ka:jti   'The white cat ate that white rat'
   white cat that white rat   ate
7. mets tʃi:t mets po:p tsu:k ka:jti   'Two cats ate two white rats'
   two cat two white rat   ate
8. məh po:ʃ   tsu:k jahʔoʔokti   'The big spider killed the rat'
   big spider rat   killed
9. mets məh tʃi:t mets məh tsu:k jahʔoʔokti 'Two big cats killed two big rats'
   two big cat two big rat   killed
10. he mets tsu:t he tsu:k ʔiʃti   'These two horseflies saw that rat'
    this two horsefly that rat   saw

13. Expanding the noun (2)

In the previous chapter we considered ways of expanding the noun with single word items: determiners and adjectives. In this chapter we turn our attention to the expansion of nouns by means of structures comprising more than one word: phrases and clauses.

Possessive phrase

Possessive phrases allow a relationship of possession to be expressed between one noun (phrase) and another noun (phrase); eg English "the big man's overcoat". The possessive phrase in English takes up the position of the identifier in the modification of the noun; more specifically, it replaces a possessive identifier, cf "his overcoat", "the big man's grey overcoat". It will be noted that the possessive noun phrase in English is marked by the possessive (genitive) case suffix *'s*. In fact, this is not a genuine suffix on the noun, since, as we noted in Chapter 9, it is attached to the last item of the possessive phrase: "the man in the corner's overcoat", "the last man out's overcoat". It is, therefore, more appropriately termed a possessive clitic.

English has an alternative means of expressing the possessive relationship: by a noun phrase introduced by the preposition *of*, placed after the noun which is possessed, eg "the tail of the aeroplane" (cf "the aeroplane's tail"). The *of*-possessive construction seems to be preferred with *aeroplane*, whereas the *'s*-clitic construction seems preferred with *man*, cf "the grey overcoat of the big man". In general, nouns referring to persons prefer the premodifying position in English, unless the noun being possessed is itself heavily modified, eg "the grey overcoat of the big man with the bowler hat talking to the lady in the fur-coat". Contextual factors also play a part in the choice of possessive construction in English.

Few languages have the luxury of a choice of possessive phrase. In Punjabi, for instance, there is one way of forming a possessive phrase, which is a kind of synthesis of the two English means. Punjabi has postpositions instead of the prepositions of English: the possessive phrase is formed by means of the postposition *da* after the possessor noun (phrase). The possessive phrase (ie noun phrase *da*) is positioned in the premodifying position of the noun being possessed, eg "mwnde di kytab" (*lit.* 'boy of book'), 'the boy's book'.

Consider now the followeing data (SIL 1980: G6) from Bariba (Dahomey):

1.	sabii	'Sabi'
2.	sabiin kurɔ	'Sabi's wife'
3.	durɔ	'man'
4.	durɔ wi	'that man'

69

5. durɔ boko   'the big man'
6. durɔ win kurɔ   'that man's wife'
7. durɔ bokon kurɔ   'the big man's wife'
8. durɔ geo wi   'that good man'
9. durɔ geo win kurɔ   'that good man's wife'
10. sabiin kurɔ geo wi   'that good wife of Sabi'

From Nos 4, 5 and 8 it will be noted that determiners and adjectives normally follow (postmodify) the noun in Bariba. The possessive phrase in Nos 2, 6, 7, 9 and 10, however, precedes (premodifies) the noun, which means that it does not replace one of the other modifiers. Thus in No 10, English cannot have both *that* (demonstrative identifier) and *Sabi's* (possessive phrase) as premodifiers, and has to resort to the circumlocution with the postmodifying *of*-phrase. The marker of the possessive phrase in Bariba is a clitic -*n*, attached to the last item of the phrase: to the noun in Nos 2 and 10, to the demonstrative in Nos 6 and 9, and to the adjective in No 7.

Exercise 28

Describe the expression of possession in the following Basari (Ghana) data (SIL 1980: G9):

1. ubɔti   'chief'
2. uninja bɔtiu   'man's chief'
3. unimpu   'wife'
4. uninja nimpuu   'a man's wife'
5. unimpu ubɔ   'one wife'
6. uninja-nee nimpuu ubɔ   'this man's one wife'
7. kusaau   'farm'
8. kusaau kubɔ   'one farm'
9. uninja saaku   'a man's farm'
10. uninja saaku kubɔ   'a man's one farm'
11. uninja ubɔ saaku   'one man's farm'
12. kukuntuu   'mortar'
13. u kuntuuku   'his mortar'
14. u nimpuu kuntuuku   'his wife's mortar'
15. uninja-nee nimpuu kuntuuku   'this man's wife's mortar'

Relative clause

The relative clause is a means of expanding or modifying a noun by means of a whole sentence (or predication), without the noun itself having a function in the sentence, except through a substitute. Compare in English: "the girl is eating her breakfast", "the girl who is eating her breakfast". The first of these examples is a sentence, and the noun *girl* has a function in the sentence, viz that of Subject. The second example is not a sentence (it is a noun phrase), though it contains a sentence, viz "who is eating her breakfast"; and the noun *girl* has no function in this sentence except through the substitute (pronoun) *who*. Here, then, the sentence—termed a 'clause' because it is 'subordinate' or 'embedded'—is part of the noun phrase; it modifies and expands the noun.

In English the relative clause occurs in postmodification position in the noun phrase. It is linked explicitly to the head noun by means of the noun substitute, the relative pronoun, which always occurs in initial position in the relative clause, irre-spective of its function in the clause. In the example above, the relative pronoun *who* is functioning as Subject in the relative clause, and so it occurs in its normal position in sentence structure. When relative pronouns occur with functions other than Subject, the normal structure of the sentence may be disturbed; eg in "the girl that I like best" the relative pronoun *that* functions as Object, so that the order in the clause is 'Object—Subject—Predicator . . .'. In fact, when a relative pronoun functions as Object in the relative clause in English, it may be omitted ("the girl I like best"). Note also that English has a relative pronoun that functions as a posses-sive phrase: *whose*, eg "the philosopher whose ideas I am quoting". Here, *whose ideas* is Object in the relative clause, and *whose* substitutes for *the philosopher's* as possessive phrase modifying *ideas*.

The distinction that we discussed in the previous chapter between 'defining' and 'non-defining' is relevant also to relative clauses. A relative clause may be used to define the reference of a noun; eg

"Which girl were you talking to?"
"I was talking to the girl who was wearing the red scarf."

Alternatively, a relative clause may be non-defining, providing additional, gratuit-ous information about the referent of a noun; eg

"I was talking to a girl from the team yesterday . . . . The girl, who was wearing a scarf in the team colours, was telling me . . . ."

Non-defining relative clauses in English are usually bounded by commas in writing and are intonationally distinct in speech. The same convention does not apply in written German, though, where all relative clauses are bounded by commas: "die Dame, die einen roten Halstuch trug, hat mir gesagt . . .", 'the lady who was wear-ing a red scarf told me . . .' or 'the lady, who was wearing a red scarf, told me . . .'.

In Hindi, a relative clause, together with the noun that it is modifying, often pre-cedes the sentence in which the noun phrase has a function (as Subject, Object, etc). The noun modified by the relative clause is then 'picked up' in the main sen-tence by a 'correlative' pronoun, eg

"jis   admi ne yah patr   likha, vah bhartiy hoga"
 who man   this letter wrote he   Indian probably-is,

ie 'The man who wrote this letter is probably an Indian'. In fact, the rule seems to be that definite nouns modified by relative clauses are placed before the main sen-tence, while indefinite nouns modified by relative clauses are placed after the main sentence, cf

"maim ek admi se bat kar raha tha jo   kal   bharat jaega
 I   a   man to   talk cont. was who tomorrow India   will-go,

ie 'I was talking to a man who is going to India tomorrow'. The so-called 'relative-correlative' construction in Hindi includes a greater variety of structures than just relative clauses.

Consider now the following data (SIL 1980: G1) from Konkomba (Ghana):

1. u ba kpo   'He died'
   he past die
2. bi   ba   kan uwon   'They saw the rabbit'
   they past see rabbit
3. bi   ba   kan uwon u n ba   kpo na   'They saw the rabbit which died'
   they past see rabbit it   past die
4. unambuun ba   gɛɛn   'The cat slept'
   cat   past sleep
5. u   ba   fii   'He/It got up'
   he/it past get-up
6. unambuun u n ba   gɛɛn na ba   fii   'The cat which slept got up'
   cat   it past sleep   past get-up

The relative clause is placed immediately after the noun that it modifies. The modified noun is represented in the relative clause by the 3rd person singular pronoun *u*; in both examples, this functions as Subject in the relative clause. The relative clause is marked by the particles *n* and *na*: *n* occurs after the Subject pronoun, and *na* occurs clause-finally.

Non-finite clauses

One of the functions of non-finite clauses (ie clauses containing a non-finite verb form—infinitive or participle) in some languages is to modify nouns; eg in English "the girl looking at the book", "the accident witnessed by the people at the bus stop", "the person to see about your problem". In English, non-finite clauses postmodify the noun. In German, where they occur less frequently, they generally premodify the noun if they are participle clauses; eg "der den Ball mit der Hand berührende Fussballspieler" (*lit.* 'the the ball with the hand touching footballer'), ie 'the footballer touching the ball with his hand'; "die an der Haltestelle angehaltene Strassenbahn" (*lit.* 'the at the stop stopped tram'), ie 'the tram stopped at the stop'. Note that the participles come finally in the non-finite clause, next to the noun being modified, and that they then inflect like adjectives. If the non-finite clause is an infinitive clause, it postmodifies the noun in German, eg "die Fähigkeit, das Klavier zu spielen" 'the ability to play the piano'.

Since, unlike relative clauses, non-finite clauses generally lack a sentence element, viz the Subject, the relationship of the modified noun to the clause is not made explicit. In fact, the modified noun is the implied Subject of the non-finite clause, at least of participle clauses: in the case of a present participle clause, the Subject of an active clause ("the girl looking at the book"—"the girl is looking at the book"); and in the case of a past participle clause, the Subject of a passive clause ("the accident witnessed by the people at the bus stop"—"the accident was witnessed …"). The relationship of a noun to a modifying infinitive clause is more problematical. In "the person to see about your problem", the modified noun *person* would appear to be the implied Object of the infinitive clause, cf "(you) see the person about your problem". But in "the first person to discover oxygen", the modified noun *person* is implied Subject in the infinitive clause ("the person discovered oxygen"). And in "the ability to play a musical instrument", the modified noun *ability* has no recognisable implied function in the infinitive clause: *ability* is derived from the adjective *able*, or rather from the verb *be able*, so that the noun phrase is perhaps relatable to the sentence "someone is able to play a musical instrument".

Exercise 29

In the following data (SIL 1980: G11) based on Agatu (Nigeria), describe the possessive phrase and the relative clause:

1. ɔi   wa   'The child came'
   child came
2. ewo wa   ɔlɛ   ɛnɛ   'The dog came to the compound yesterday'
   dog came compound yesterday
3. ada   wa   ɛnɛ   'Father came yesterday'
   father came yesterday
4. ɔi   ma ewo ɛnɛ   'The child saw the dog yesterday'
   child saw dog yesterday
5. ada gɔi ɛpa wa ɛnɛ   'The father of the two children came yesterday'
            two
6. ɔi ma ewo gada   'The child saw the father's dog'
7. ɔi ma ewo ɛpa   'The child saw two dogs'
8. ada ma ewo ɛpa gɔi   'Father saw the child's two dogs'
9. ɔi ma ɔlɛ   'The child saw the compound'
10. ada gɔlɛ ma ɛhi gɔi   'The compound-head (father-of-compound) saw the
              pot   child's pot'
11. ewo ma ɔi gada gɔlɛ   'The dog saw the compound-head's child'
12. ewo ɛpa gada gɔlɛ wa ɛnɛ   'The compound-head's two dogs came yesterday'
13. ada ma ɔi ni   wa ɛnɛ   'Father saw the child who came yesterday'
                who
14. ada ma ewo ɛpa gɔi ni wa ɛnɛ 'Father saw two dogs of the child who came yesterday'
15. ɔi ma ewo ɛpa ni wa ɛnɛ   'The child saw the two dogs that came yesterday'
16. ɔi ni wa ɛnɛ ma ɛhi ɛpa   'The child who came yesterday saw two pots'
17. ɔi ni ma ɛhi ɛpa gada gɔlɛ wa 'The child who saw the compound-head's two pots
    ɛnɛ   came yesterday'

14. Expanding adjective and adverb

Not all languages, as we noted in Chapter 12, have separate classes of adjective and adverb (cf the Apinaye data in Exercise 5). Or, as in German, there may be considerable overlap between identifiable classes of adjective and adverb. Nevertheless, it is often possible to identify different functions corresponding to those of the adjective and the adverb in English, ie modifier of nouns (cf Chapter 12) or Complement (cf Chapter 11) for adjectives, and Adjunct (cf Chapter 11) for adverbs.

In this chapter we want to look at ways in which adjectives and adverbs may be expanded. The possibilities of expansion are severely limited by comparison with those for nouns.

Intensifiers

In many languages, adjectives and adverbs may be expanded by a set of words known as intensifiers, themselves often regarded as a subclass of adverbs. The representative intensifier in English is *very*, eg in "very beautiful", "very quickly". In fact, *very* only ever functions as an intensifier in English, as does the equivalent word in French, *très*. In German, however, *sehr* may function alone as an Adjunct as well as in combination with an adjective or adverb as intensifier, eg "es regnet sehr" 'it's raining a lot', "sehr schön" 'very beautiful(ly)'. Not all words functioning as intensifier in English are restricted to that function, cf *absolutely* as intensifier in "His suggestion is absolutely marvellous", and as Adjunct in "I repudiate his accusation absolutely".

In the *Grammar of Contemporary English* (Longman 1972), Quirk *et al* identify three classes of intensifier in English, in recognition of the fact that some 'intesifiers' have the opposite function to that indicated by their label; ie there is in fact a scale of intensification. The three classes of intensifier are those of: emphasisers, amplifiers, and downtoners. It should be pointed out that some intensifiers in English have functions other than those of expanding adjectives and adverbs. The following examples will serve to illustrate the classes of intensifier in the expansion of adjective/adverb in English: emphasiser—"definitely shut"; amplifier—"completely clean", "thoroughly badly"; downtoner—"rather flat", "moderately important", "hardly new", "almost illiterate". It will be noted that intensifiers in English are generally placed before the adjective or adverb they modify, though *enough* is an exception to this rule, cf "bad enough".

Not all adjectives and adverbs in English may be expanded by means of an intensifier. In the case of adjectives, it is the so-called 'gradable' adjectives that may be readily expanded in this way, ie adjectives with a 'more-or-less' meaning rather than an 'either/or' meaning. For example, *bad* is a gradable adjective, since there are degrees of badness: something may be "more bad" or "less bad", or indeed "very bad", "completely bad" or "fairly bad". On the other hand, *wooden* is not a gradable adjective, since something either is made of wood, or it is not; so that we cannot talk of *"a very wooden toy", for example. Sometimes, though, intensifiers are used with non-gradable adjectives, when they have an 'emphasising' function, cf the "definitely shut" example above, or the much criticised expression "very unique".

In the case of adverbs, it is the set of conjunctive adverbs, like *however*, *therefore*, *moreover* and *besides*, which may not be expanded by means of intensifiers. Also, the set of pro-form adverbs—*here*, *there*, *now*, *then*—do not normally occur with intensifiers, though there are ways in English of 'emphasising' these adverbs, eg "right here", "just then".

To illustrate the intensification of adjectives in another language, consider the following data (based on SIL 1980: D8) from Tataltepec (Mexico):

1. ngatsi late? bi?   'That cloth is yellow'
   yellow cloth that
2. ngatī ʃi   kiña?ā late?   'Many cloths are fairly white'
   white fairly many
3. tlju ʃi ñatī   bi?   'That person is fairly large'
   big   person
4. tlju tsa: ska ?uru   'One donkey is very big'
   big very one donkey
5. tlju tsa: 'It is very big'
6. ngatī tsa: late? tlju re   'This big cloth is very white'
                    this
7. ndi?ī   tsa: ñatī   'There were lots of people'
   there-was lots

Most of the sentences in this data are based on a C-S pattern, without a Predicator. Adjectives like *ngatī* 'white', *tlju* 'big' may be expanded by intensifiers such as *ʃi* 'fairly' and *tsa:* 'very', which are placed after the adjectives they modify. Note that *tsa:* also has a function as a quantifier in the expansion of a noun (No 7), ie as a member of the same class as *ska* 'one' and *kiña?ā* 'many'.

Comparative expressions

Another way of expanding adjectives and adverbs is by means of comparative expressions. This kind of expansion is possible with the same sets of adjectives and adverbs that may be subject to intensification. Comparative expressions involve on the one hand either an appropriate (eg comparative) form of the adjective or a comparative adverb, and on the other some kind of comparative phrase or clause; eg "worse than we had imagined", "the most beautiful jewel in the whole world".

In English, 'more/less' comparison has either a noun phrase introduced by the preposition *than* or a clause introduced by *than* as a conjunction, eg "bigger than an elephant", "less frequent than the timetable states". Superlative expressions ('most/least' comparison) have either a locative expression or a clause introduced by conjunction *that*, eg "the least expensive in the shop", "the most reliable that money can buy". There is a similar expression in English with *too* and an infinitive clause, eg "too tired to walk another step"; and also a comparative expression of 'equality' with *as* either as preposition or as conjunction, eg "as foolish as the next man", "as foolish as I thought he would be".

All the examples so far have been with adjectives. Similar expressions occur also with adverbs, eg "more gracefully than I have ever seen", "most patiently of all the prisoners", "too decisively to be ignored", "as quickly as he was able". And similar expressions can be found in other European languages at least; eg French "plus fort que son frère" 'stronger than his brother', "plus vite que je ne le croyais" 'faster than I thought' (note the insertion of *ne* 'negative particle' and the pronoun *le* 'it' in the comparative clause); German "so kalt wie es im Januar war" 'as cold as it was in January', "zu müde, einen weiteren Schritt zu machen" 'too tired to take another step'.

In Punjabi there are no comparative or superlative forms of the adjective as in English or German. Comparison relies on the use of the comparative particle equivalent to English *than*: *toŋ* or *naloŋ*. For example:

"mwn̪ḍa kwṛi toŋ ləmma e"   'The boy is taller than the girl'
  boy   girl than tall   is
"o məythoŋ syan̪e e"   'He is cleverer than me'
he me-than clever is

With the superlative, the quantifying pronoun *səb* 'all' is used with the comparative particle; eg

"é kər   da səb toŋ cənga kəmra e"   'This is the best room in the house'
this house of all than good room is

Note that the phrase in this last example is a possessive phrase (*kər da*) rather than a locative phrase as in English, cf German "das grösste Zimmer des Hauses", lit. 'The biggest room of the house'.

In the Hixkaryana language of Brazil (cf Desmond C Derbyshire, *Hixkaryana*, North Holland 1979), there are three ways of expressing the comparative relation. The first is by juxtaposing a negative and a positive clause!

eg "kawohra naha Waraka.   kaw naha Kaywerye"
  tall-neg he-is   tall he-is

which could be translated either as 'Waraka is not as tall as Kaywerye', or as 'Kaywerye is taller than Waraka'. The second is by juxtaposing positive clauses containing 'degree' particles like *nyhe* 'more', *rmahaxa* 'very much':

eg "ohxe naha meku.   ohxe nyhe naha yayhɨ.ohxe rmahaxa   naha honyko"
  good it-is monkey   more   tapir   very-much   peccary

ie 'Monkey is good, tapir is better, and peccary is really good'.

The third means is by the use within the clause of postpositional relators *-oho* 'bigger than, more important than' and *-osnaka* 'less than, smaller than':

eg "kratxatxa yoho naha tukusu"
  grasshopper bigger-than it-is humming-bird

'The hummingbird is bigger than the grasshopper'

"enahɨ yoho rmahaxa tɨnyahke natxow hamɨ"
eating-of-it greater-than very-much having-food they-are 'deductive'

'It is evident that they have much more food than they can eat'.

Adjectives—phrasal/clausal expansion

One further way of expanding adjectives—in English at least, though it is probably by no means universal—is by means of a phrase or a clause. The type of phrase concerned is a prepositional phrase (ie noun phrase introduced by a preposition), eg 'fond of cream cakes", "anxious about the future", "annoyed at the suggestion". It will be noted that particular adjectives are associated with specific prepositions; compare further "keen on ice hockey", "different from his brother", "disgusted with the exam result", "contrary to all advice", "eager for new experiences". With some adjectives the noun phrase which the preposition introduces may be replaced by an *-ing*-clause (clause introduced by a present participle form of the verb) or by a *wh*-clause (introduced by a '*wh*' word, eg *what, who, when*), eg "guilty of robbing the bank", "uncertain about what they should do next", "angry about where the telephone had been put".

The clausal expansion of adjectives in English is by means of a *that*-clause or an infinitive clause, eg "concerned that nothing would be done", "anxious to arrive at work on time", "eager to please everybody", "important that nothing should be forgotten". Adjectives that are expanded in this way, and indeed by means of a prepositional phrase, may only function predicatively in English, usually after the verb *be*. It is arguable that '*be* + adjective' should thus be regarded as a verb, which is what the equivalent would be in some languages, cf *be afraid*—German *sich fürchten*.

Exercise 30

Describe the expansion of adjectives in German from the following data. Note that German has a four-term case system: nominative (nom), accusative (acc), genitive (gen) and dative (dat):

1. Er war seinen Eltern gehorsam   'He was obedient to his
     he was his(dat) parents obedient   parents'
2. Wir wollen unserer Sorgen ledig sein   'We want to be free of our
     we want our(gen) troubles free to-be   troubles'
3. Er ist zu dieser Aufgabe fähig   'He is capable of this task'
     he is to this(dat) task capable
4. Sie ist gegen dieses Medikament empfindlich   'She is allergic to this
     she is against this(acc) medicine allergic   medicine'

5. Dieses   Haus ist nicht den   Preis wert
   this(nom) house is not   the(acc) price worth
   'This house is not worth the price'

6. Er ist es müde, dauernd   zu arbeiten
   he is it   tired   continually to-work
   'He is tired of continually working'

7. Sie ist von seiner Unschuld überzeugt
   she is of   his(dat) innocence convinced
   'She is convinced of his innocence'

8. Sie ist auf die   Leistung   stolz
   she is on the(acc) achievement proud
   'She is proud of the achievement'

9. Er ist für den   Schaden haftbar
   he is for the(acc) damage responsible
   'He is responsible for the damage'

10. Er ist damit einverstanden, dass wir sein   Auto borgen
    he is it-with agreeable   that we his(acc) car   borrow
    'He is aggreable to us borrowing his car'

15. Locatives and temporals

Two of the most common kinds of circumstantial information that we choose to specify for any event are 'where' the event took place and 'when' it took place; that is, 'locative' information and 'temporal' information, respectively. Location and time are, however, not simple concepts. In the case of location, for example, one may specify the place 'at' which an event takes place, or the place 'towards' or 'from' which movement occurs, besides the position of things relative to each other (eg 'in front of', 'behind', 'beside', 'below', etc). Similarly in the case of time, one may specify the point in time 'at' which an event occurred, or the amount of time that an event took up (duration), or the relative distribution in time of events (eg 'before', 'after', 'while'). Another fairly common kind of circumstantial information that is specified is the Manner in which an event takes place or an action is carried out, answering the question "How did it happen?" or "How was it done?". Other kinds of circumstantial information include: purpose, cause, reason, result, condition, etc.

Such information usually occupies the Adjunct slot in sentence structure (see Chapter 11). In this chapter we shall consider the various grammatical means for expressing circumstantial information, in particular locative and temporal information.

Adverb phrases

Adverb phrases are relatively abbreviated forms of locative and temporal expression, consisting often of only a single adverb without intensification. Sometimes, especially in the case of locatives, they have a pro-form function, referring back in a text to a fuller expression of location or time by means of pre/postpositional phrases or adverbial clauses (see below). This is particularly true in English, for example, of the adverbs *here*, *there*, *now* and *then*. Other locative adverbs in English include the adverb particles like *in*, *out*, *below*, *above*, *behind*, as in sentences like "Push the knob in", "We'll clamber below", "Another bus is coming behind".

Besides *now* and *then*, other point-of-time adverbs in English include *today*, *yesterday* (though in some contexts these might be considered to be nouns), *soon*, *just*, *afterwards*, *before*. There are also time-frequency adverbs such as: *often*, *sometimes*, *occasionally*, *frequently*, *usually*, *again*, *never*. Most commonly expressed by adverb phrases, in English at least, is Manner: all the adverbs formed from adjectives by the addition of the derivational suffix *-ly* are manner adverbs, eg *gracefully*, *quietly*, *happily*, *beautifully*, *slowly*, *candidly*, as in "She danced gracefully", "They moved quietly", "The children play very happily together".

Consider now the adverb phrases in the following data (SIL 1980: E2), based on Northern Pueblo Totonac (Mexico):

1. waɬ
   he-spoke
2. tʃuʔnca nawan
   thus   he-will-speak
3. waɬ maqɬuwa
        many-times
4. tʃoʔla   waɬ lakapaɬ
   probably   quickly
5. tʃuʔnca wan qaʔwa:ʔtʃu laqali nawan
              the boy   tomorrow
6. nawan maqɬuwa laqali tuʃumaʔn   'He will speak many times in the future'
              day-after-tomorrow
7. pedro waɬ laqa:tʃu
   Peter   everywhere
8. qo:tan   pedro ki:waɬ   wampala
   yesterday   went-to-speak again
9. a:kalista:n nawan pedro lakapaɬ
   after-that
10. nawan laqa:tʃu ka:cisa:t
                   early
11. waɬ aʔca maqɬuwa
        here

The locative adverbs in this data are: *laqa:tʃu* 'everywhere', *aʔca* 'here'. The temporal adverbs are, firstly time-when: *laqali* 'tomorrow', *tuʃumaʔn* 'day-after-tomorrow', *qo:tan* 'yesterday', *a:kalista:n* 'after-that', *ka:cisa:t* 'early'; secondly time-frequency: *maqɬuwa* 'many times', *wampala* 'again'. The manner adverbs are: *tʃuʔnca* 'thus', *lakapaɬ* 'quickly'. *tʃoʔla* must also be considered as an adverb, perhaps belonging to a class of 'modal' adverbs (cf Chapter 17).

Prepositional/postpositional phrases

We have encountered pre/postpositional phrases already, eg in the expansion of adjectives (Chapter 14), and in the expansion of nouns (Chapter 13). Here we consider them functioning as Adjunct with locative, temporal and other circumstantial meanings. In 'prepositional' phrases the particle precedes the associated noun (phrase), eg English "in the garden"; whereas in 'postpositional' phrases the particle follows the associated noun (phrase), eg Punjabi "bəzar yc" (*lit.* 'bazaar in') 'in the bazaar'. Not all languages have pre/postpositional phrases (eg Turkish), but rely instead on a system of cases in the noun, so that nouns or noun phrases in the appropriate case signal locative/temporal information. Other languages (eg Latin, German) have a system of prepositions governing the case of the associated noun; eg German "in die Stadt" (*in* + accusative) 'to the town', "in der Stadt" (*in* + dative) 'in the town'.

Pre/postpositional phrases as Adjunct express primarily locative and temporal information. Examples of locative prepositional phrases in English are: "The incident occurred *outside the swimming baths*", "The children are playing *in the garden*", "Grandpa is asleep *on the sofa*". And examples of directional phrases: "We're going *into the town centre*", "They raced *across the park*", "We've just come *from the cricket match*". Here are now some examples of temporal prepositional phrases in English, firstly time-when phrases: "The incident occurred *in the morning*", "We all went to sleep *after our lunch*", "The manager can see you *at any time during the day*". Secondly, time-frequency/duration phrases: "They made the noise *throughout the afternoon*", "The voyage lasted *for six days*". Time-duration is also expressed by noun phrases, without preposition, in English; eg "The performance lasted *four hours*", "They were at sea *ten days*". Time-when is also expressed in this way with days of the week and the like, eg "The accident happened *last Friday*", "We shall go to Greece *next Spring*".

Prepositional phrases perform a similar function of expressing locative/temporal information when they occur in the expansion of nouns, eg "the house on the corner", "the discussion after lunch", "my thoughts during the lecture". But prepositional phrases as modifiers of nouns do not always perform this function; sometimes a noun requires a particular preposition + noun (phrase) as a kind of complement, eg "his request for asylum", "her annoyance at the rumours", where *for* and *at* are not replaceable by any other preposition but are determined by the nouns *request* and *annoyance*, respectively.

Exercise 31

Describe the locative and temporal expressions in the following data (SIL 1980: E4) from Bekwarra (Nigeria):

1. a kà ye ká
   he then went there
   'Then he went there'

2. a maŋ ye ká
   again
   'He went there again'

3. a be kɨn
   came here
   'He came here'

4. a kà maŋ be
   'Then he came again'

5. a be ufufo
   yesterday
   'He came yesterday'

6. a ye ká ufufo
   'He went there yesterday'

7. a be yè ká
   from
   'He came from there'

8. a kà ye yè kɨn
   'Then he went from here'

9. a ye k' utyen ufufo
   to farm
   'He went to the farm yesterday'

10. a ci kɨn yè ufufo
    stayed
    'He has stayed here since yesterday'

11. a ne uni   ká
    saw   someone
    'He saw someone there'

12. a kà maŋ ne he ká
              him
    'Then he saw him there again'

Temporals and the verb phrase

Clearly, temporal expressions, particularly referring to time-when, frequently have the function of amplifying or making more specific the tense marked in the verb phrase. So, in the sentence "They arrived yesterday", the -(e)d of *arrived* indicates the point in time at which the event occurred as being past, and the temporal adverb *yesterday* makes that point in time specific. In Urdu, the word for 'yesterday' is the same as the word for 'tomorrow'; the distinction is provided by the tense of the verb. Compare:

"kəl   kya dyn tha?"   'What day was it yesterday?'
yesterday which day it-was
"kəl   kya dyn hoga?"   'What day will it be tomorrow?'
tomorrow   it-will-be

Likewise, the same word is used for 'the day before yesterday' and for 'the day after tomorrow', viz *pərsoŋ*.

The reverse situation obtains in English with some expressions of future time, where the burden of future reference rests solely with the temporal expression; eg in "They are visiting the museum *tomorrow/on Friday/next week*", where the tense is 'present progressive', and the absence of the temporal expression would remove reference to future time. A similar dependence on the temporal expression occurs with the simple present tense, eg "They visit the museum *tomorrow*"; though here the removal of the temporal expressions creates a gap that is appropriately filled by a time-frequency expression, eg "They visit the museum *every week/on Wednesdays*".

Time-frequency meanings in English may be expressed within the verb phrase without the presence of a temporal expression. Compare: "He always bangs the door when he comes in", with the temporal adverb *always*, and "He will bang the door when he comes in", where a similar meaning is expressed by the modal auxiliary verb *will*. A similar expression is the use of *keep on* in sentences like "He kept on banging the door", in which *keep on* could be regarded as some kind of auxiliary verb.

Consider also the meanings of frequency and repetition expressed in different verb forms in the following data (from SIL 1980: A23) from Tlingit (Alaska):

1. nagúttʃ   'he goes frequently'
2. a xsatíntʃ   'he sees it often'
3. askóowtʃ   'he always knows'
4. yoo sya.átk   'they go back and forth'
5. a daa yoo toowatánk   'he's thinking something over'
6. at únt   'he's shooting (repeatedly)'
7. a klaxútt   'he's splitting (firewood)'
8. datátʃt   'he's clapping (in time to music)'

Adverbial clauses

There is a further, more expansive means of expressing locative, temporal and indeed all kinds of other circumstantial information: adverbial clauses. Like adverb phrases and pre/postpositional phrases they can be regarded as having the function of Adjunct in sentence structure, though in this case it is a matter of 'embedding' one clause in another clause (see Chapter 19). Adverbial clauses are frequently introduced by conjunctions, which specify the circumstantial meaning of the clause, eg in English *where* for locative adverbial clauses ("The accident happened *where the two roads meet*"), *when* for temporal point-of-time adverbial clauses ("*When you come home* I shall have the meal ready").

Temporal adverbial clauses may be particularly important for indicating the time relationship between two events, eg by means of adverbial clauses introduced by the conjunctions *before*, *after*, *while* ("*Before they went to bed* they washed and brushed their teeth", "They went to bed *after they had washed and brushed their teeth*", "*While they were brushing their teeth* the telephone rang"). This is not the only clausal means of indicating the temporal relationship between events, however, neither in English nor in other languages: a participle clause, without a conjunction, may serve a similar purpose, eg "*Having washed and brushed their teeth*, they went to bed", "*Brushing their teeth*, they heard the telephone ring". There must, however, be an identity of reference between the implied Subject of the participle clause and the actual Subject of the main clause (cf "Brushing their teeth, the telephone rang").

Consider now the following data (from SIL 1980: F13) from Xavante (Brazil), where the temporal relator is not a conjunction, but a suffix in the verb of the adverbial clause:

1. tete madaa-wamhã   te mo   'When he had watched it, he
   he watched-it-when he went   went'
2. tete upra-re   wa mada   'I watched while he bought it'
   he bought-it-while I   watched
3. te mañari-mono-re   tetete upra   'Whenever I made it, he bought
   I   made-it-habitually-while he   bought-it-   it'
                                     habitually
4. tete upsõ-mono-wamhã   tete madaa   'Whenever he washed it, I
   he washed-it-habitually-when I   watched   watched'

Note that the adverbial clause appears always to take up initial position in the sentence.

Adverbial clauses may serve to express several further kinds of circumstantial information, besides locative and temporal. For example: cause or reason, introduced by *because* or *since* in English; condition, introduced by *if* or negatively by *unless*; concession, introduced by *although*; result, introduced by *so that*; purpose, introduced by *in order that* or simply an infinitive clause ("Jack and Jill went up the hill *to fetch a pail of water*"). Eg "He arrived late, *because his car broke down*", "*If you agree to my suggestion*, I will help you", "The museum is shut, *so that we cannot visit it today*".

Exercise 32
Describe the adverbial clauses in the following Finnish data (SIL 1980: F1):
1. ostin   auton   'I bought a car'
   I-bought car

2. rikastuin   'I became rich'
3. elin rikastunut   'I had become rich'
4. rikastuttuani ostin auton   'Having become rich, I bought a car'
5. kun elin   rikastunut ostin auton   'When I became rich, I bought a car'
   when I-had

6. rikastun   'I am becoming/will become rich'
7. jos rikastun ostan auton   'If I become rich, I will buy a car'
   if   I-buy

8. menin kaupunkiin   'I went to town'
   I-went to-town

9. menin kaupunkiin ostamaan auton   'I went to town to buy a car'
                    to-buy

16. Agreement

Items in a linguistic unit that are in some kind of syntactic relationship, eg Subject and Predicator in a sentence, adjective and noun in a noun phrase, may mark that relationship in some way. We noted, too, in previous chapters how, in German, prepositions are followed by nouns in a specific case, eg *von* 'of, from' by the dative, *für* 'for' by the accusative (see further below). Items that are in a syntactic relationship and have that relationship marked are said to be 'in agreement'. In this chapter we shall consider the kinds of syntactic relationship that are marked and the means employed for marking them, ie the kinds of 'agreement' that occur in languages.

Noun phrase

Items in the noun phrase—determiners, adjectives, nouns—are frequently found to be 'in agreement'. Consider the English noun phrase "these girls": by comparison with the singular form "this girl", it can be seen that both demonstrative (*this—these*) and noun (*girl—girls*) are marked for 'plural' number. There is agreement between demonstrative and noun in respect of number, marked (in the spoken form) in the demonstrative by the lengthening of the vowel ($\imath \rightarrow$ i) and voicing of the final sibilant (s $\rightarrow$ z), and marked in the noun by the addition of the suffix /z/. This is probably the only kind of agreement that can be found in English noun phrases.

Consider now the following examples of French noun phrases:

1. le bon garçon   'the good boy'
2. les bons garçons   'the good boys'
3. la bonne fille   'the good girl'
4. les bonnes filles   'the good girls'

Taking the written forms for our description—the description of the spoken French forms would be much more complex—it is clear that there is agreement between article, adjective and noun in respect of 'plural' number (Nos 2 and 4), marked by the -*s* suffix on each item (additionally there is a change of vowel in the article in No 4, as compared with No 3, from *a* to *e*). In addition, there is agreement between the three items in respect of gender (*garçon* is a 'masculine' noun, *fille* is a 'feminine' noun), marked in the article by the alternation between *le* and *la*, marked in the adjective by the addition of -*ne* for feminine gender, but not marked in the noun, which may be regarded as having inherent gender. In Nos 2 and 4, then, we may say that there is agreement in respect of both gender and number between article, adjective and noun, marked in the ways indicated.

When we turn to German we find agreement in the noun phrase, not only in respect of number and gender, but additionally in respect of case. The German noun (phrase) has a three-term gender system ('masculine', 'feminine' and 'neuter') and a four-term case system ('nominative', 'accusative', 'genitive', 'dative'). Consider the following paradigms for the noun phrases "der gute Mann" 'the good man', "die gute Frau" 'the good woman', and "das gute Boot" 'the good boat':

		Masculine	Feminine	Neuter
sing	nom	der gute Mann	die gute Frau	das gute Boot
	acc	den guten Mann	die gute Frau	das gute Boot
	gen	des guten Mannes	der guten Frau	des guten Bootes
	dat	dem guten Mann	der guten Frau	dem guten Boot
pl	nom	die gute Männer	die guten Frauen	die guten Boote
	acc	die guten Männer	die guten Frauen	die guten Boote
	gen	der guten Männer	der guten Frauen	der guten Boote
	dat	den guten Männern	den guten Frauen	den guten Booten

It will be noted that there is by no means maximal differentiation of forms; there is in fact considerable overlap, eg the -en form of the adjective (guten) appears throughout the plural paradigms and in a good number of cases in the singular ones. Similarly the article form die occurs in nominative and accusative in all three genders in the plural, in addition to the feminine singular in those two cases. It should, however, be pointed out that the form of the adjective depends on the kind of determiner present, and whether a determiner is present or not, cf "ein guter Mann" (nominative singular), "guter Männer" 'of good men' (genitive plural). A principle of economy appears to be at work in these paradigms, requiring the clear marking of gender, number and case once only in each noun phrase.

Consider now the following data (SIL 1980: C2) from Basari (Ghana), set as *Exercise 7* in Chapter 3:

1. uni umbini   'this person'   biniib bimbini   'these persons'
2. ubɔti umbini   'this chief'   bibɔtiib bimbini   'these chiefs'
3. diyin dimbini   'this name'   ayin ŋimbini   'these names'
4. dibil dimbini   'this seed'   abil ŋimbini   'these seeds'
5. kusaau kumbini   'this farm'   tisaati timbini   'these farms'
6. kukabuu kumbini   'this basket'   tikabuti timbini   'these baskets'

As we saw in Exercise 7, the noun and the demonstrative are marked by means of prefixes and suffixes according to gender (1, 2 and 3) and number (singular and plural) in the following way:

		Noun	Demonstrative
Gender 1			
-bɔti 'chief'	sing	u-	u-
-ni 'person'	pl	bi- -ib	bi-
Gender 2			
-yin 'name'	sing	di-	di-
-bil 'seed'	pl	a-	ŋi-
Gender 3			
-saa- 'farm'	sing	ku- -u	ku-
-kabu- 'basket'	pl	ti- -ti	ti-

That is to say: there is agreement between noun and demonstrative in respect of gender and number, marked by affixes as shown in the table above.

Exercise 33

Describe the agreement in the Portuguese noun phrase from the following data (SIL 1980: C3). The order of elements is: demonstrative—noun—adjective.

1. esse menino gordo   'that fat boy'
2. essa menina bonita   'that pretty girl'
3. esses meninos gordos   'those fat boys'
4. essas meninas bonitas   'those pretty girls'
5. esse vestido bonito   'that pretty dress'
6. essa galinha gorda   'that fat hen'
7. esses vestidos bonitos   'those pretty dresses'
8. essas galinhas gordas   'those fat hens'

Sentence

We turn now to agreement within the sentence. Here the agreement usually involves the marking of a syntactic relationship between the Predicator and some other sentence element, often the Subject. Compare the following pair of sentences in English: "My son plays chess"—"My sons play chess". The difference between singular and plural is marked in both the Subject and the Predicator, in the singular by the absence of -*s* in the Subject noun with corresponding presence of -*s* in the verb, and in the plural by the presence of -*s* in the Subject noun with corresponding absence of -*s* in the verb. Thus, we can say that there is agreement between Subject and Predicator in English with respect to number, marked by the presence/absence of an -*s* suffix as outlined above. However, this agreement applies only to 3rd person Subjects and only in the presence tense, except for the verb *be* (cf "I am/you are/he is", "I/he was/you were").

In written French, on the other hand, as we saw in Chapter 4, there is consistent agreement in respect of person and number in all tenses, marked by suffixes in the verb, with little duplication of forms. A similar extensive agreement obtains between Subject and Predicator in German; cf the following present tense paradigm for *gehen* 'go':

	Singular	Plural
1st person	ich gehe	wir gehen
2nd person	du gehst	Ihr geht
3rd person	er/sie/es geht	Sie/sie gehen

In Gujerati transitive sentences the Predicator agrees with the Object, in some instances in respect of gender, number and case, in others in respect of gender and number only. For example (from W S Tisdall, *Gujerati Grammar*, New York: Ungar 1961):

1. "E baie vagaḍamañ dahaḍa kahaḍya", 'That lady passed her days in the wilderness'. Here *kahaḍya* 'passed' is in the 'absolute' case, 'plural' number, 'masculine' gender, to agree with *dahaḍa* 'days'.

2. "Tene e rajae pakaḍyo", 'The king seized him'. Here *pakaḍyo* 'seized' is masculine singular, to agree with *tene* 'him', but it is in the 'absolute' case while *tene* is in the 'oblique' case with -*ne*.
3. "Teṇe Raṇine ranmadañ nasaḍi muki", 'He removed the queen into a forest'. Here the verb *muki* is in the feminine singular, agreeing with the Object *Raṇi* 'queen', though *Raṇi* is in the 'oblique' case with -*ne*.

Consider now the following data (SIL 1980: C9) from Tsonga (South Africa/Mozambique):

1. mufana watlaŋga	'The boy plays'
2. mufana lonkulu watirha	'The big boy works'
3. mufana watɛka	'The boy laughs'
4. mufana watsutʃuma	'The boy runs'
5. mufana wadja	'The boy eats'
6. mufana wadja ʃihari leʃikulu	'The boys eats the big animal'
7. βafana βatlaŋga	'The boys play'
8. βafana laβakulu βatirha	'The big boys work'
9. βafana βatɛka	'The boys laugh'
10. βafana βatsutʃuma	'The boys run'
11. βafana βadja	'The boys eat'
12. ʃihari ʃatsutʃuma	'The animal runs'
13. ʃihari leʃikulu ʃabaleka	'The big animal runs away'
14. sihari satsutʃuma	'The animals run'
15. sihari lesikulu sabaleka	'The big animals run away'

In this data there is agreement both within the noun phrase (Nos 2, 6, 8, 13, 15) and within the sentence. Agreement in the sentence is between Subject and Predicator with respect to gender and number, marked by prefixes in the Subject noun and in the verb as follows:

		Subject	Predicator
Gender 1			
-fana 'boy'	sing	mu-	wa-
	pl	βa-	βa-
Gender 2			
-hari 'animal'	sing	ʃi-	ʃa-
	pl	si-	sa-

The agreement in the noun phrase is between noun and adjective, with respect to number and gender, marked by prefixes as follows:

		Noun	Adjective	
Gender 1	sing	mu-	lon-	(No 2)
	pl	βa-	laβa-	(No 8)
Gender 2	sing	ʃi-	leʃi-	(Nos 6, 13)
	pl	si-	lesi-	(No 15)

Concord and government

Sometimes in the discussion of agreement a distinction is made between two kinds of agreement: 'concord' and 'government'. The distinction refers to the way in which agreement is marked. In the case of concord, all the items in agreement are marked in some way. So, in the Tsonga data just considered, both Subject and Predicator are marked by prefixes in the sentence agreement, and in the noun phrase agreement both noun and adjective are marked by prefixes. So, these are both instances of concord.

Government, then, refers to the type of agreement where not all items are marked: one item, the unmarked one, is said to 'govern' the form of the other items in the syntactic unit. In the French singular noun phrase, for example (cf "la bonne fille", 'the good girl'), the noun is not itself marked for gender (though it belongs to the 'feminine' gender), but it governs the form (feminine) of the article *la* and the adjective *bonne*. Things are complicated in the plural noun phrase, however, because 'plural' number is marked in all the items in the unit (cf "les bonnes filles"). Perhaps a too rigid insistence on the distinction between concord and government will in some cases be descriptively unhelpful. How, for example, could one fit the agreement in English "The boy plays"/"The boys play" into this distinction?

Pre/postpositions

As we have seen before (cf Chapter 15) prepositions or postpositions are often associated with nouns in a particular case. This could be considered a form of government: a pre/postposition governs the case of an associated noun. Sometimes pre/postpositions in a language all govern the same case; eg in Punjabi, postpositions are preceded by nouns in the 'oblique' case, or in English if a preposition governs a personal pronoun it is in the 'object' case (cf "to me", "for him", "from us").

In other languages (eg German) the situation is more complex. Some prepositions in German always govern the same case, eg *von* ('from', 'of') + dative, *für* ('for') + accusative, *wegen* ('because of') + genitive. The majority of prepositions are of this kind. A few prepositions, however, may govern more than one case, usually with a difference of meaning; eg *in* ('to', 'towards', 'into') + accusative, *in* ('in', 'inside') + dative; *auf* ('onto') + accusative, *auf* ('on', 'on top of') + dative.

Exercise 34

Describe the agreement in the following data (SIL 1980: C10) from Mbembe (Nigeria):

1. oñi   ope   'The elephant died'
   elephant died
2. ojinɔŋ ope   'The man died'
   man
3. eten   eze ojinɔŋ   'The animal saw the man'
   animal saw
4. ajinɔŋ maze eten ndoma   'The men saw this animal'
   men   saw   this

5. ojinɔŋ ŋwoma oze nten   nta:n
      this   saw animals three

'This man saw three animals'

6. ajinɔŋ mboma ata:n maze nten njoma nta:n
      these   three   these

'These three men saw these three animals'

7. ajinɔŋ ata:n mape
           died

'Three men died'

8. nten njoma nta:n ipe
               died

'These three animals died'

9. oñi ŋwoma ope za
            there

'This elephant died there'

10. añi   mboma ata:n mape za
    elephants

'These three elephants died there'

11. ojinɔŋ ŋwoma oze añi mboma za

'This man saw these elephants there'

17. Mood and voice

In this chapter we consider two grammatical categories that are commonly associated with the verb phrase, but which also often have implications for sentence ordering and structure. The category of 'mood' is frequently understood to involve two separate sets of distinctions, on the one hand the contrast between declarative/affirmative, interrogative, negative, imperative and perhaps subjunctive, and on the other hand the expression of notions such as necessity, probability and certainty, and of such notions as obligation, ability and volition. The category of 'voice' refers primarily to the distinction between 'active' and 'passive', though some languages distinguish also a 'middle' voice.

Interrogative mood

In discussing the interrogative and other such moods, the assumption is usually made that the declarative or affirmative mood is somehow basic, and interrogative, negative, etc, sentences are derived from declarative ones. Mood is sometimes referred to as 'sentence modification'. Essentially, moods concern the role which a speaker takes on in relation to a proposition, ie as questioner, requestor, commander, denier, etc. Languages vary in the ways in which moods are realised grammatically, whether morphologically or syntactically.

It is useful to distinguish two kinds of interrogative sentence: 'polar' questions and 'information' questions. Polar questions ask merely about the polarity (negative/positive) of a proposition, and so they expect the answer "Yes" or "No", eg in English "Have you let the cat out?" Information questions, on the other hand, ask for some specific information and include an information-seeking word (interrogative pronoun, adverb or adjective) which identifies the specific information, eg in English "*Who* is your brother talking to?", "*Where* did you put my scissors?" Here *who* is an interrogative pronoun that expects a noun (phrase) for an answer, and *where* is an interrogative adverb that expects an Adjunct of some kind for an answer.

In English, interrogative mood is realized largely by syntactic rearrangement. This is certainly true in the case of polar questions, which are formed from declarative sentences by the inversion of Subject and first auxiliary verb in the verb phrase, eg "You have let the cat out" → "Have you let the cat out?" If there is no auxiliary verb in the verb phrase of the declarative sentence, then the dummy auxiliary *do* is used in the question, eg "You gave Susan the book" → "Did you give Susan the book?" In information questions in English the information-seeking word is placed first in the sentence, followed by the first auxiliary verb, then the Subject, the remainder of the verb phrase and the rest of the sentence, eg "My brother has been talking to the headmaster" → "Who has my brother been talking to?" Here the information-seeking word (interrogative pronoun *who*) is functioning as the Object of *talk to*. If the interrogative word is functioning as Subject, then the syntactic rearrangement described does not apply, eg "My brother has been talking to the headmaster" → "Who has been talking to the headmaster?"

A similar kind of realization of interrogative mood applies in French, eg "Vous avez acheté un cadeau pour votre mère" ('You have bought a present for your mother') → "Avez-vous acheté un cadeau pour votre mère?" ('Have you bought ...'), "Jean a acheté un cadeau" ('John has bought a present') → "Qui a acheté un cadeau?" ('Who has bought a present?'). French, however, has an alternative way of asking questions that does not involve syntactic rearrangement of the declarative form, but instead the use of an interrogative particle (*est-ce que* for polar questions) placed initially in the interrogative sentence, eg 'Est-ce que vous avez acheté un cadeau?" ('Have you bought a present?'). The interrogative particle may also be used in information questions with an interrogative pronoun, eg "Qu'est-ce que Jean a acheté?" ('What has John bought?'), but this would appear to be restricted to Object interrogative pronouns.

Consider now the following data (SIL 1980: F10) from Bimoba (Ghana):

1. a   ŋaapoo daa   jeet daak   ni 'Your wife bought food in the market'
   your wife   bought food market in
2. a bik la   jeet le   'Where did your child see food?'
   child saw   where
3. a   daa jeeta   'Did you buy food?'
   you   food-?
4. n bik kɔi ti   naab   'My child sold our cow'
   my   sold our cow
5. a sa   kɔi be   daak ni   'What will you sell in the market?'
   will   what
6. a baa   kɔi na naab daak nia   'Did your father sell the cow in the market?'
   father   the   in-?

From this data it would appear that in Bimoba polar questions are formed by simply adding an interrogative clitic *-a* to the last item in the sentence (Nos 3 and 6). Information questions are formed by substituting the appropriate item with an appropriate interrogative word, without any syntactic rearrangement: *le* 'where' in Adjunct position in No 2; *be* 'what' in Object position in No 5. It is worth pointing out that we have not discussed the role of intonation in signalling interrogative mood, either in this data or any other examples we have considered.

Negative mood

The term 'negative' contrasts with 'affirmative' and implies the denial of a proposition. In English, negative mood is realized primarily by the negative particle *not*, which is placed after the first auxiliary in the verb phrase, eg "Bill is mending the car" → "Bill is not mending the car". If the verb phrase contains no auxiliary verb, then the dummy *do* is used in negative sentences, eg "Bill mends cars" → "Bill does not mend cars". This is by no means the only way of making an affirmative sentence negative in English, as this sentence (using *by no means*) and the *if*-clause in the previous sentence (using negative determiner *no*) illustrate. English, in common with many other languages, also has a number of negative pronouns and adverbs that realize negative mood, eg *nobody*, *nothing*, *nowhere*, *never*.

In German, which is also endowed with negative pronouns and adverbs, the negative particle *nicht* is placed at the end of the sentence if it is negating the whole sentence, but before a particular item if that is the focus of negation; eg "Hans repariert Autos nicht" ('Hans does not repair cars'), "Hans repariert nicht Autos, sondern Fahrräder" ('Hans doesn't repair cars but bicycles'). In French, the negative particle is, as in English, associated with the verb phrase; and it is in two parts, *ne ... pas*, eg "Il n'a pas acheté un cadeau" ('He has not bought a present'). French, however, rather than having a set of negative pronouns/adverbs, has a number of negative particles: *ne ... personne* 'nobody', *ne ... rien* 'nothing', *ne ... jamais* 'never'; eg "Je ne connais personne" ('I don't know anybody'/'I know nobody'), "Je ne l'ai jamias vu" ('I have never seen him'). Because of its position, one might count *never* as a negative particle in English, along with *not*.

Consider now the following data (part of SIL 1980: E15) from Mbembe (Nigeria):

1. ojinɔŋ okpe aji   'The man sells palm nuts'
2. ojinɔŋ aji kokpe   'The man does/did not sell palm nuts'
3. ojinɔŋ okpe ogwu sa ɛp̃ya   'The man sells corn in the market'
4. ojinɔŋ ogwu sa ɛp̃ya kokpe   'The man does/did not sell corn in the market'
5. ojinɔŋ oto   'The man falls'
6. ojinɔŋ koto   'The man does/did not fall'
7. ojinɔŋ ope   'The man dies'
8. ojinɔŋ kope   'The man does/did not die'

From this data it would appear that negative mood in Mbembe is realised by the prefix *k-* on the verb word and the shifting of the verb to sentence-final position, if it does not already occupy that position. The distinction between present and past tense appears to be neutralised in negative mood.

Imperative and subjunctive moods

In the imperative mood the speaker takes on the role of one who gives an order or command: "Bring me the newspaper". In English, imperative mood is signalled by the use of the base (or bare infinitive) form of the verb and the omission of the Subject (an implied 2nd person pronoun *you*). In French it is the 2nd person present tense forms of the verb that are used in imperative sentences: "Viens" ('Come here'), "Allez" ('Go away'). The same is true of German, except that here the infinitive may also be used to signal imperative mood, especially in public contexts, eg "Bitte festhalten" ('Hold tight, please').

In English the use of the imperative to issue a command sounds rather formal and abrupt, even when tempered by *please*; an imperative implies an asymmetric status relationship between speaker (higher status) and addressee (lower status). In symmetric relationships commands or requests are often issued by means of an interrogative sentence, eg "Will/Can/Would you bring me the newspaper?", or even by means of a declarative sentence, eg "I'd rather like the newspaper". For this reason it is probably important to distinguish mood (as a grammatical category) from sentence function (as a semantic/pragmatic category), since they are not necessarily in a one-to-one relationship.

In the subjunctive mood a speaker casts doubt on the validity or veracity or reality of the proposition he is making. In English, the subjunctive survives only in a few fossilised phrases like "If I were you . . ."; its function has been taken over by the modal verbs *should* and *would*. In French, the subjunctive verb form is found in subordinate clauses after certain verbs of cognition, eg *croire* 'believe', *vouloir* 'want'/'wish': "Je crois qu'elle soit morte" ('I believe her to be dead'), "Je veux qu'il vienne" ('I want him to come'). The subjunctive is also associated with other moods or roles that a speaker may adopt, eg wishing, cf English "Long live the Queen", "God bless you", where the verb form lacks the usual *-s* suffix of the 3rd person singular present. With the subjunctive and its expression of doubt and uncertainty we have come close to the other set of distinctions under the heading of 'mood', sometimes also called 'modality', to distinguish it from the set we have so far considered.

Exercise 35

Describe the signalling of interrogative mood in the following data (SIL 1980: F9) from Yakurr (Nigeria):

1. odam   owu okoh kebla   'Your husband has gone to the farm'
   husband your go   farm
2. odam owu okoh kebla-o   'Has your husband gone to the farm?'
3. umana-wahm oyahu kah   'My friend is there'
   friend-my   is   there
4. umana-wahm oyahu kah-o   'Is my friend there?'
5. na   yakehw yati etehn   'They are going to kill an animal'
   future they-go kill animal
6. na yakehw yati etehn-o   'Are they going to kill an animal?'
7. wol   liweh litahwa   'He is well'
   body his   is-strong
8. wol liweh litahwa-o   'Is he well?'

Mood—modality

We turn now to the second set of meanings associated with the term 'mood', but also called 'modality'. Again we are concerned with a role, or stance or attitude that a speaker takes up in relation to the proposition that he is making. In this case, however, the speaker intervenes with his assessment of the possibility, probability or certainty of the proposition. One way in which English expresses these kinds of meanings is by means of the so-called 'modal' auxiliary verbs: *can, may, must, will, shall*. For example, "The letter may come tomorrow", "It could come tomorrow", "It will come tomorrow", "It must come tomorrow" express varying degrees of certainty/uncertainty or possibility concerning the proposition. But the modal auxiliary verbs are not the only means of expressing these modal meanings in English: there is, for example, a set of modal adverbs (or modal particles) that may be added to a sentence to modify the proposition in respect of its certainty or possibility: *maybe*, *perhaps*, *for sure*, *certainly*, *possibly*, *probably*, etc; eg "Perhaps the letter will come tomorrow", "The letter will come tomorrow for sure".

Some of these modal adverbs also have adjective and noun counterparts, eg "It is possible that the letter will come tomorrow"—"There is a possibility that the letter will come tomorrow", "It is certain that the letter will come tomorrow". Thus English realises the meanings of modality in a number of ways. French, on the other hand, does not have the same range of modal auxiliary verbs as English, but more often uses adverbs and adjectives to express modality; eg "Il vient demain *peut-être*", 'He may come tomorrow'/'Perhaps he'll come tomorrow'.

Consider now the following data (SIL 1980: E13) from Tlingit (Alaska), presented in a modified form as Exercise 25 in Chapter 11:

1. xóots   shakdé saxwaa.áx   dzeeyáak   ʾMaybe I heard a brown bear
   brown-bear   voice-I-heard earlier-on   earlier on'
2. Juneau-dé kwshé kukgwaatèen   'Perhaps he's going to Juneau
                   he-will-take-a-trip   on a trip'
3. kúnaxkusi.áat' xáa   'It's sure cold'
   really it-is-cold
4. tlax a yáanax   ee wdixwétl kwshé   'Maybe you're too tired'
       it face-beyond you is-tired
5. ee   xòonee kwshé   'Maybe it's your friend'
   your friend
6. aatlèin dáanaa xáa doo jèewoo   'He sure has lots of money'
   lots   money   his hand-loc.

The underlined items represent modal particles (adverbs or perhaps modal auxiliary verbs); they appear to be positioned before action verbs (Nos 1 and 2) but after state verbs (Nos 3 and 4), but they can also occur in verbless clauses (Nos 5 and 6).

Modal verbs in English have another set of meanings (permission, ability, obligation) which are arguably not a matter of mood or modality, unless one views these meanings as extensions of the primary possibility/certainty meanings of the modals. The distinction has been made between the speaker or discourse-oriented uses of the modals (ie speaker's assessment of possibility or certainty) and the subject-oriented uses (ie permission, obligation, etc) as in: "Can you ride a bicycle?", "You may leave now", "We must report to the police tomorrow".

Passive voice

When we turn to 'voice' we are considering not so much the speaker's assessment of or attitude to what he is saying, but rather the speaker's choice of the way in which he presents, within the sentence, the elements of his proposition. Voice, then, is concerned not so much with the speaker's relationship to his proposition or his interlocutor, but to the text of which the proposition forms a part, whether that text is a monologue or a dialogue. On the other hand, the term 'passive' has a further connotation, namely that the Subject of the sentence is being acted upon, rather than being the actor.

In a passive sentence the Object of the active sentence becomes the Subject, and the Subject of the active sentence takes a subordinate position in an 'agent'-phrase, while the verb is put into the passive form (in English, *be* followed by past participle). For example, the English active sentence "A bus hit the car" transforms into the passive sentence "The car was hit by a bus", where *the car* is Object in the active sentence but Subject in the passive, and *a bus* is Subject in the active sentence but in the 'agent'-phrase "by a bus" in the passive. In English it is possible to leave the Agent unexpressed, ie to omit the agent-phrase, eg "The drivers of the two vehicles were killed". The passive transform is thus only possible for active sentences that contain an Object, ie are transitive. But this is, in fact, not the whole story of the passive in English: see Exercise 36 below.

The passive is particularly important in a language like English, where the order of sentence elements is relatively fixed, since the syntactic function (Subject, Object, etc) is largely defined by position. In a language with a well developed case system that distinguishes the syntactic function of sentence elements, a passive structure is not so important from a textual point of view. In German, for example, which does have a passive construction, the rearrangement of sentence elements can be achieved without recourse to the passive, eg "Mein Freund besuchte meinen Vater" ('My friend visited my father')—"Meinen Vater besuchte mein Freund" (*lit.* 'My father (accusative) visited my friend (nominative)'), ie 'My father was visited by my friend'. German differs from English also in that an 'impersonal' passive is possible that is not relatable to an active sentence with an Object, eg "Es wurde getanzt" (*lit.* 'it was danced'), ie 'There was dancing'.

In Punjabi the passive is used considerably less frequently than in English and normally in an agentless construction, eg "ethe pənjabi boli jandie e" (*lit.* 'here Punjabi spoken Passive is'), ie 'Punjabi is spoken here'. In tenses formed with the past participle (past, perfect, past perfect, future perfect) transitive verbs have a special construction (in the active) that is superficially equivalent to the English passive construction, as follows: the Subject is put in the oblique case and is followed by the postposition *ne* 'by', the participle agrees in gender and number with the Object; eg "mwnḍe ne pənjabi sykkhi e" (*lit.* 'boy by Punjabi learnt is'), ie 'The boy has learnt Punjabi'.

Middle voice
Some languages, eg Ancient Greek, have for some verbs in some tenses separate forms for active, passive and middle voice. If active voice implies as Agent doing an action, and passive voice implies a Patient undergoing an action, middle voice implies a person/thing acting of its own accord or in its own interest. The distinctions may be illustrated by the following English sentences:

1. Harry opened the door   — active
2. The door was opened by Harry   — passive
3. The door opened   — middle.

In English, middle voice (if No 3 can be so termed) is not marked by a distinct form of the verb: the Patient/Undergoer of the action occurs as Subject (as in the passive example—No 2), but the verb is in the 'active' form (cf No 1). In other languages (eg German, French) the verb in No 3 would be in a reflexive form, eg German "Die Tür öffnete sich" (*lit.* 'the door opened itself'). This kind of reflexive has, however, to be distinguished from reflexives that refer to an action that an Agent does to itself, eg "Sie wäscht sich" ('She's washing herself'), which must be regarded as active in voice.

Exercise 36

Describe the passive voice in English as illustrated by the following sentences:

1. They were arrested by the border police.
2. Everyone who reaches 100 is sent a telegram by the queen.
3. A telegram is sent by the queen to everyone who reaches 100.
4. The trial will be held next month.
5. It is understood that a statement will be made this evening.
6. This bed was slept in by Queen Victoria.
7. The garden has been walked over.
8. Hundreds of people are killed every year in road accidents.

18. Embedding (1)

The syntactic phenomenon that we shall discuss in this and the following chapter is very widespread in the world's languages and is indeed probably universal. It is referred to by a number of terms in grammatical description: subordination, rankshifting and embedding are three such terms, of which we shall use the last. By embedding we mean the function of a syntactic unit as a constituent of a unit the same size (at the same rank or level) as itself, or its function as a constituent of a unit smaller (at a lower rank) than itself. For example, a sentence is regarded as being composed of words and their accompanying expansions (ie phrases); but if a sentence functions as a constituent of another sentence, then we will say that it is 'embedded'. Similarly, phrases are regarded as being composed of words; but if a phrase functions as a constituent of another phrase, we will say that it is 'embedded'. In this chapter we consider phrases that are embedded in other phrases, and in the next chapter we consider embedded sentences.

Possessive phrases

We have discussed possessive phrases already (Chapter 13) in the context of the expansion of nouns. Possessive phrases are, then, constituents of noun phrases; that is to say, they have the same kind of function (expansion or modification of nouns) as, say, an adjective—a unit of word rank. Since they function like words, in the composition of phrases, we regard possessive phrases as being embedded.

Consider the following English noun phrase containing a possessive phrase: "the little girl's new toy". The noun that is being expanded is *toy*, and it is expanded by the adjective *new* and the possessive phrase *the little girl's*. Thus the possessive phrase has the same status in relation to *toy* as the adjective word *new*: it is a phrase functioning like a word; it is a phrase embedded within another phrase, a possessive noun phrase within a noun phrase. The possessive phrase can, then, in turn, be considered as the expansion of a noun: *girl*, expanded by the adjective *little* and the identifier (article) *the*. We can show these relationships by means of a tree-diagram type of display:

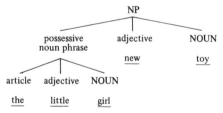

We then need to note that the embedded possessive noun phrase is marked as such by the possessive clitic -'*s* attached to the final item of the possessive phrase.

The alternative possessive construction in English—by means of the *of*-phrase placed after the noun being expanded—is like any other prepositional phrase expanding a noun in English. These are considered below. But here let us deal with the Punjabi possessive construction that we discussed in Chapter 13: "mwnḍe di kytab" (*lit.* 'boy of book'), 'the boy's book'. Here too the possessive phrase *mwnḍe di* is to be regarded as embedded, since it, as a whole, expands the noun *kytab*:

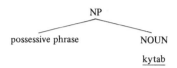

However, since *di* is a postposition, the possessive phrase in Punjabi, like the *of*-phrase in English, falls into the category of pre/postpositional phrases, which are discussed below.

Exercise 37

Describe the structure of the noun phrase in the following data (SIL 1980: G19) from Ngbaka (Zaire), including any embedding:

1. mi zɔ   kɔla
   I   saw chicken
   'I saw a chicken'

2. gā kɔla bɔa yɔa
   big   two lost
   'Two big chickens are lost'

3. kɔla 'da wele yɔa
        of man
   'The man's chicken is lost'

4. be   kɔla 'da mi yɔa
   small   of me
   'My small chicken is lost'

5. kɔla 'da kpasa wele yɔa
        old   man
   'The old man's chicken is lost'

6. kuli 'da kɔla bɔa fɛnga
   egg   white
   'The eggs of the two chickens are white'

7. kuli nalɛ 'da a   fɛnga
        four   him
   'His four eggs are white'

8. a oso   kɔla nalɛ 'da wuko
   he bought   woman
   'He bought the woman's four hens'

Prepositional/postpositional phrases

We discussed pre/postpositional phrases earlier (Chapter 15) in the context of their function as locatives and temporals, as Adjuncts in sentence structure and as modifiers of nouns. We will discuss pre/postpositional phrases in the context of embedding from two points of view. Firstly, as we noted previously, pre/postpositional phrases are most often composed of a noun and any expanding or modifying items (ie a noun phrase) and an accompanying preposition or postposition. The pre/postposition is not regarded as part of the expansion of the noun, but is viewed as relating to the noun and its expansion as a whole. Seen in this way, a prepositional phrase is composed of a preposition and a noun phrase, ie PrepP = Prep + NP. The noun phrase is thus a constituent of the prepositional phrase and can be said to be embedded in it. The noun phrase embedded in prepositional phrases has the same structure as non-embedded noun phrases.

To illustrate this last point, consider the following data (part of SIL 1980: G8) from Engenni (Nigeria):

1. ɔmu   bo kirikiri   'all big houses'
   house big all
2. ade   ya na ɔmu bo   'Father is at the big house'
   father is at
3. edei bo kirikiri ya na ɔmu   'All the big men are at the house'
   men
4. adide   kirikiri nyeni na ɔmu bo   'All rich men live in big houses'
   rich-man   live
5. owutumu ya na ɔmu do kirikiri   'Rats are in all the old houses'
   rats   old

Here the prepositional phrases (preposition *na* + NP) are functioning as Adjunct, and the noun phrase shows the same variety of structure whether functioning as Subject or embedded in the prepositional phrase (compare Nos 2 and 4, Nos 3 and 5).

The second point to be made about pre/postpositional phrases and embedding is that they may themselves be embedded in other phrases. For example, when a prepositional phrase functions (as a modifier) in the expansion of a noun in English it is embedded in the noun phrase, eg "the old shed in the garden". Here, *in the garden* is a prepositional phrase expanding *shed* and thus has the same function as the adjective (word) *old* in the noun phrase. The relationship of embedding may be made plain by showing the structure of the noun phrase in a tree-diagram type of display:

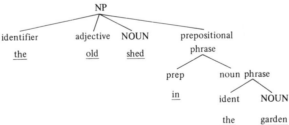

This display plainly shows the prepositional phrase as a constituent of the noun phrase which is the expansion of the noun *shed*, and the noun phrase *the garden* in turn as a constituent of (ie embedded in) the prepositional phrase.

Clearly, possessive phrases in English formed with the preposition *of* ("the windows of the train") or in Punjabi formed with the postposition *da* (see above) are embedded in the same way in their noun phrases. With this kind of expansion of nouns (ie by means of pre/postpositional phrases) it is possible to find multiple embedding: a noun in a noun phrase embedded in a prepositional phrase may itself be expanded by a prepositional phrase. Consider the following data (SIL 1980: G10) from French:

1. le   gros chien
   the big dog
2. le gros chien de la petite fille
              of the little girl
3. le gros chien de la petite fille de l'épicier
                    of the grocer
4. la   soupe chaude
   the soup hot
5. la soupe chaude de la   vieille femme
            of the old   woman
6. une goute de la soupe chaude de la vieille femme
   a   drop of

In No 3, for example, the prepositional phrase *de l'épicier* expands the noun *fille* (ie is embedded in that noun phrase), and *de la petite fille* itself is embedded in the noun phrase which is the expansion of *chien*. We can display these relationships in a tree-diagram as follows:

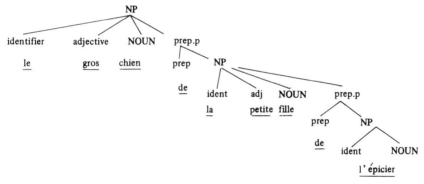

Adjective phrases

We shall consider adjective phrases in the context of embedding from two points of view: firstly, adjective phrases as phrases embedded in other phrases; and secondly, adjective phrases as phrases containing embedded items. We discussed adjectives as items expanding nouns in Chapter 12, and we discussed the expansion of adjectives themselves in Chapter 14, but we have not brought the two together. That is, we have not yet considered the role of expanded adjectives (ie adjective phrases) in the expansion of nouns. Consider the following English noun phrase: "a very large elephant". Here the noun *elephant* is expanded by the identifier (article) *a* and by the adjective phrase *very large*. The word (intensifying adverb) *very* is not part of the expansion of the noun *elephant* but of the adjective *large*: the adjective phrase is thus embedded in the noun phrase, as the following tree-diagram shows:

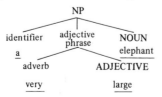

The same relationship obtains in all languages where a noun may be expanded by an adjective which is itself expanded by an intensifying adverb: cf German "ein sehr grosser Hund", 'a very big dog'; French "une fille très jolie" (*lit.* 'a girl very pretty'), 'a very pretty girl'.

The second point about adjective phrases and embedding is that the expansion of an adjective may itself contain an embedded item. When we discussed the expansion of adjectives in Chapter 14, we noted that it could contain phrases (eg prepositional phrases) and sentences (eg non-finite clauses, 'that'-clauses). Consider the following English example: "very fond of cream cakes". Here the adjective *fond* is expanded by the intensifying adverb *very* and by the prepositional phrase *of cream cakes*. The prepositional phrase is, therefore, regarded as embedded in the adjective phrase, as the following tree-diagrams shows:

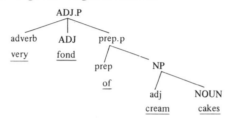

As discussed above, the prepositional phrase, in turn, may be viewed as containing an embedded noun phrase. Consider now the following English adjective phrase: "very annoyed that Harry was late". It has a similar structure to the one just considered, except that in this case the embedded item is a 'that'-clause rather than a prepositional phrase:

With this example we are encroaching on the topic of the next chapter, which deals with the embedding of sentences.

Exercise 38

Describe the embedding to be found in the following data (SIL 1980: G14) from Tampulma (Ghana). Notes: 1. *-u* is added to the final word of a sentence if it ends in a consonant; 2. the final vowel of all words is elided, except the last in a phrase.

1. mu la   tɔhɔn-u   'I am going to the village'
   I   go-to village
2. koor zennyɛn tɔhɔn ni   'The tall chief lives in the village'
   chief tall lives   in
3. koor zen dama zen-u   'The tall chief's house is large'
            house large
4. koor dam   zen nyɛn tɔhɔn ni   'The chief's large house is in the village'
        house   is
5. mu nyɛn koor zen dam zen ni   'I live in the tall chief's large house'
      live
6. koor nyɛn tɔhɔn zen ni   'The chief lives in the large village'
        lives

19. Embedding (2)

Sentences in phrases

In this chapter we turn our attention to the embedding of sentences, and we begin by considering the embedding of sentences in phrases. A common embedding of this type is that of relative clauses in the expansion of noun phrases, discussed earlier in Chapter 13. Consider the following English example: "the tall mechanic who is repairing my car". This noun phrase is the expansion of the noun *mechanic*, by means of the adjective word *tall*, the identifier (article) *the*, and the relative clause *who is repairing my car*. The relative clause thus has the same function in the expansion of the noun as the adjective or the identifier; it is a sentence with a word-like function in the composition of the noun phrase. It is functioning at a rank lower than itself; it is an embedded sentence. A relative clause in English has the same structure as an independent sentence, except that one element is replaced by a relative pronoun that represents within the relative clause the noun being expanded. The relationships are made clear by presenting the structure in the form of a tree-diagram type of display:

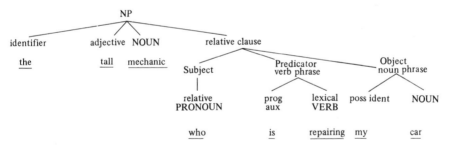

In this example, the relative pronoun *who* functions as Subject in the embedded relative clause. Consider now an example which includes the relative pronoun *whose*: "the manager whose name I have forgotten":

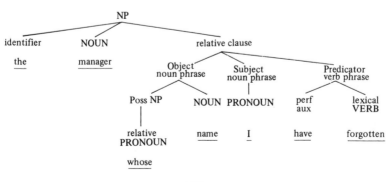

103

Here the relative pronoun, *whose*, is functioning as part of the expansion of the Object noun phrase, namely as a possessive noun phrase. So, *whose* is embedded as a possessive phrase in the expansion of the noun *name*, which constitutes the Object of the embedded relative clause.

Let us now illustrate relative clauses further by considering some data (SIL 1980: G16) from Ngbaka (Zaire):

1. a   so   li
   she drew water

   'She drew water'

2. wuko   tɛ   do   katini   bɔa
   woman came with bucket two

   'The woman brought two buckets'

3. wuko kɛ a sua li ni tɛ do katini bɔa

   'The woman who drew water brought two buckets'

4. be   to   ka
   child pound fufu

   'The child pounded fufu'

5. be kɛ a tua ka ni mbɔkɔ
                        is-tired

   'The child who pounded fufu is tired'

6. wa   tɛ̀   he   mɔ
   they cont cried thing

   'They were crying'

7. mi zɔ   be bɔa kɛ wa tɛ̀ hia mɔ ni
   I   saw

   'I saw two children who were crying'

8. be te
       fell

   'The child fell'

9. be kɛ a tia ni he mɔ

   'The child who fell cried'

Here the relative clause is marked by boundary particles: *kɛ* initially, and *ni* finally. The item in the relative clause that corresponds to the noun being expanded is replaced by a 3rd person pronoun: *a* 'singular' (Nos 3, 5, 9), and *wa* 'plural' (No 7). The verb in the relative clause has a special form: *sua* instead of *so*, *hia* instead of *he*. The relative clause is an embedded sentence, as in English; the structure of the Object noun phrase in No 7 can be displayed in a tree-diagram as follows:

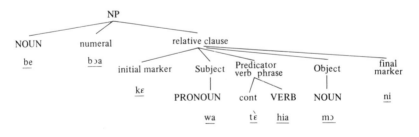

The other kind of sentence or clause that we discussed in Chapter 13 in the context of the expansion of nouns was the non-finite clause, a sentence containing an infinitive or participle form of the verb, as in: "the boy riding his bicycle down the road". Like the relative clause, the non-finite clause is a sentence embedded in a noun phrase, though, as we mentioned in Chapter 13, a sentence that usually does not contain a Subject. We should note too that the expansion of adjectives (cf Chapter 14) may also contain embedded sentences, eg "afraid to cross the road", "determined that the bus should run on time", where an infinitive clause is embedded in the adjective phrase of the first example, and a 'that'-clause in the second. In the case of the 'that'-clause, the conjunction *that* functions as a marker of the embedded sentence, like *kɛ* for the relative clause in the Ngbaka data considered above; it has no function in the sentence itself.

Sentences in sentences

We turn now to the embedding of sentences as elements in other sentences, functioning at the same rank as themselves. Sentences may function as Subject, Object, Complement or Adjunct in another sentence, though embedded sentences are most frequently found in the Object function. Consider the following English examples:

1. It is strange that she has not written to us.
2. She will not tell us what the doctor said to her.
3. The problem will be crossing the swollen river.

In the first example there is an embedded sentence as Subject, viz the 'that'-clause. The Subject is not in its usual initial position because English generally extraposes Subjects that are embedded sentences and fills initial position with a place-holding dummy *it*. The structure of this sentence is: 'It'—Predicator (*is*)—Complement (*strange*)—Subject ('that'-clause). Again, the conjunction *that* is merely a marker of the embedded sentence and has no function in the sentence itself.

In the second example there is an embedded sentence as Object, viz the so-called 'wh'-clause ("what the doctor said to her"). The 'wh'-clause begins with a wh-word (eg *who, what, when, where, why* and also *how*), which, unlike the *that* of 'that'-clauses, does have a function within the embedded sentence, in this case as Object of *said*. 'Wh'-clauses are sometimes called 'nominal relative' clauses, since they can be related to noun phrases of the type "that which . . .", "the person who . . .", "the time when . . .", etc, which are analyseable as noun/pronoun + relative clause. Example 2 has the structure: Subject (*she*)—Predicator (*will not tell*)—Indirect Object (*us*)—Direct Object ('wh'-clause), which can be displayed in a tree-diagram as follows:

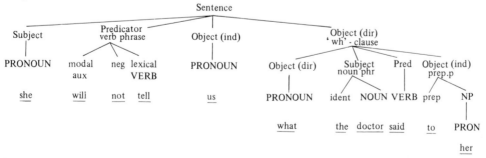

In the third example there is an embedded sentence as Complement, viz the present participle clause ("crossing the swollen river"). This is a non-finite clause and lacks a Subject. This example has the structure: Subject (*the problem*)—Predicator (*is*)—Complement (*-ing*-clause). Sentences embedded in other sentences in

English may thus be either finite, like the 'that'-clause or the 'wh'-clause, or non-finite, like the present participle (*-ing*) clause.

Consider now the following data (SIL 1980: G3) from Quichua (Ecuador) (*Note*: the 3rd person morpheme in the verb word is the suffix *-n*):

1. atun wamracunata ricun   'He/she saw the big boys'
   big boys-object   see
2. warmi yacuta   apamun   'The woman brought the water'
   woman water-obj bring
3. apamun   'He/she brought it'
4. warmi yacuta apamuj atun wamracunata   'The woman bringing the water saw
                                                       the big boys'
5. apamuj ricun   'The one bringing it saw them'
6. wamracuna mullijonta pugllanacun   'The boys are playing marbles'
   boys   marbles   are-playing
7. warmi wamracuna pugllanacujta ricun   'The woman saw the boys playing'
8. yacuta apamuj wamracuna mullijonta   'The one bringing water saw the boys
   pugllanacujta ricun   playing marbles'

In this data there are instances of embedded sentences as Subject and as Object. Note first of all that the Object marker in Quichua is the suffix *-ta*, which appears on the Objects *wamracuna-ta* 'boys' in No 1 and *yacu-ta* 'water' in No 2. This marker also occurs on the verb word of an embedded sentence functioning as Object, eg *pugllanacuj-ta* 'are playing' in No 7 and in No 8. The verb is the final element in the sentence, since the order of elements in the Quichua sentence appears to be: Subject—Object—Predicator. When a sentence is embedded, as Subject or as Object, the 3rd person suffix *-n* is replaced by the suffix *-j*, which precedes the Object marker *-ta* in the case of an embedded sentence as Object, eg *apamu-j* in Nos 4 and 5, *pugllanacu-j-ta* in Nos 7 and 8.

The embedded sentences in this data are these. In No 4 "warmi yacuta apamuj" is an embedded sentence functioning as Subject of *ricun* 'see'; it differs from the non-embedded sentence of No 3 only in the verb-final suffix *-j*. No 5 also has an embedded sentence as Subject: "apamuj", meaning 'he/she bringing it', where both Subject and Object pronouns are unrealised. In No 7 there is an embedded sentence as Object: "wamracuna pugllanacujta", which has the embedded sentence marker *-j* and the Object marker *-ta* verb-finally. Finally, No 8 has an embedded sentence as Subject and as Object: "yacuta apamuj" as Subject, "wamracuna mullijonta pugllanacujta" as Object, both marked in the ways we have discussed. The structure of No 8 can be displayed in a tree-diagram as follows:

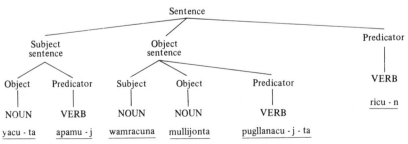

Exercise 39

Describe the embedded sentences in the following data (SIL 1980: G2) from Paumarí (Brazil):

1. 'ojoina   'I return'
2. 'i'omani   'You lie down'
3. ihai-ra   'inofimania   'Do you want medicine?'
    medicine-obj you-want-?
4. sipatihi-ra   'inofimania   'Do you want bananas?'
    bananas-obj
5. 'i'omani-ra 'inofimania   'Do you want to lie down?'
6. 'ojoina-ra 'onofivini   'I want to return'
7. sipatihi-ra 'ihaki   'You eat bananas'
         you-eat
8. sipatihi-ra 'ihaki-ra 'inofimania   'Do you want to eat bananas?'
9. 'ogorana-ra   'onajahavini   'I clean my house'
    my-house-obj I-cause-to-make-clean
10. 'ogorana-ra 'onajahavini-ra 'onofivini   'I want to clean my house'

Adverbial clauses

In the previous section we discussed only embedded sentences functioning as Subject, Object or Complement. In this section we look at embedded sentences functioning as Adjunct, or 'adverbial clauses' as they are sometimes called. These are embedded sentences conveying the 'circumstantial' meanings of Adjuncts, ie time, place, manner, purpose, result, reason, etc. Consider the following English examples:

1. We will start our meal when everybody is ready.
2. Sitting on the bus I thought of a great plan.
3. He is going to Manchester to visit some friends.
4. She cannot see you because she is too busy.

In the first example there is an embedded sentence introduced by the conjunction *when* ("when everybody is ready"). It functions in the sentence as an Adjunct of time; the temporal meaning is indicated by the conjunction. Many adverbial clauses are of this type, cf No 4 with *because*: the conjunction indicates the particular circumstantial meaning that is associated with the Adjunct, in the way that prepositions often do for prepositional phrases functioning as Adjunct. The structure of No 1 is then: Subject (*we*)—Predicator (*will start*)—Object (*our meal*)—Adjunct/time (*when . . .*).

In Example 2 the embedded sentence is: "sitting on the bus", a present participle clause, functioning as Adjunct of time. It could be replaced by an adverbial clause with a conjunction, eg "While I was sitting on the bus . . ."; or a conjunction can be added to the participle clause, eg "While sitting on the bus . . .". There are restrictions on the use of present participle clauses as Adjunct in English: since the participle clause lacks a Subject, its implied Subject must be the same as that of the sentence in which it is embedded (in our example, *I*); in general they have a temporal meaning (*when, while* or *as*).

In the third example, the embedded sentence is the infinitive clause ("to visit some friends"), functioning as Adjunct of purpose. We noted earlier that infinitive clauses can be embedded sentences functioning as Subject, Object or Complement (eg "They want to visit the exhibition"—Object). When infinitive clauses are embedded as Adjunct in English, they have the meaning of 'purpose'. No 3 has the structure: Subject (*he*)—Predicator (*is going*)—Adjunct/place (*to Manchester*)—Adjunct/purpose (*to visit . . .*).

The fourth example is like the first, with an adverbial clause introduced by a conjunction (*because*) as the embedded sentence functioning as Adjunct, but in this case an Adjunct of reason. It has the structure: Subject (*she*)—Predicator (*cannot see*)—Object (*you*)—Adjunct/reason (*because . . .*), which can be displayed by means of a tree-diagram as follows:

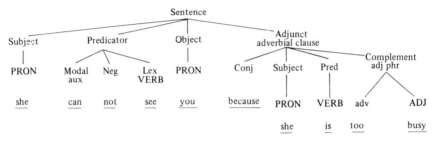

Consider now the following data (SIL 1980: G5) from Kaiwá (Brazil):

1. oheʃa gwaʔirɨ   'He saw his son'
   he-saw his-own-son
2. oho   kambɨ rehe   'He went for milk'
   he-went milk   for
3. oho jepeʔa   rehe   'He went for firewood'
       firewood
4. oho oheʃahaŋwa rehe gwaʔirɨ   'He went to see his son'
       he-see
5. ombaʔapo kokwe pɨ   'He worked in the clearing'
   he-worked clearing in
6. ou   ombaʔapohaŋwa rehe kokwe pɨ   'He came to work in the clearing'
   he-came he-work

In this data the embedded sentence functioning as Adjunct is a purpose clause (Nos 4 and 6), translated in the English gloss by an infinitive clause. In Kaiwá the purpose clause has the particle (?preposition in Nos 2, 3; ?conjunction in Nos 4, 6) *rehe* placed immediately after the verb word, and the verb word contains the suffix *-haŋwa*, which is added to the (presumably) past tense form of the verb (compare Nos 1 and 4, Nos 5 and 6).

Embedded sentences are a means of relating two propositions, such that one, represented by the embedded sentence, is marked as subordinate to or included in the other. An action or event or state of affairs may thus take on the role of Subject, or Object, or Complement, or be used to specify more fully the circumstantial information represented by an Adjunct.

Exercise 40

Describe the embedded sentences in the following data (SIL 1980: F7) from Inga (Colombia):

1. samuspa Juan micu
   coming   John ate
   'When/After/Because John came, he (John) ate it'
2. nuca samujpi Juan micu
   I   coming
   'When/After/Because I came, John ate it'
3. samuspa Juan micucu
            was-eating
   'When John came, he (John) was eating it'
4. Pedro samujpi Juan micunga
   'If Peter comes, John will eat it'
5. manara samuspa nuca micuni
   not-yet   ate
   'I ate before I came'
6. nuca manara samujpi Juan micu
                     ate
   'John ate it before I came'
7. samucuspa   Juan cahuahua
   process-of-coming   saw-me
   'John saw me while he (John) was coming'
8. nuca samucujpi   Juan cahuahua
      process-of-coming
   'John saw me while I was coming'

20. Coordination

In the previous chapter we were discussing the ways in which sentences relate to each other and to other syntactic units in a relationship of embedding, the inclusion of a sentence as a constituent in another sentence or in a phrase. We turn now to another kind of syntactic relationship that is found between sentences, and between other units as well. This is the relationship of 'coordination'. Coordination is essentially an 'and'-relationship; though other conjunctions are often counted among the coordinating ones, in English especially *or* and *but*. Coordination is not a relationship of inclusion like embedding, but a relationship of juxtaposition. In coordination, neither of the units is subordinate to or dependent on the other; both are independent, and merely joined together in a relationship of coordination.

Sentence + sentence

In English, sentences are characteristically coordinated by the conjunction *and*, although, as we noted above, *or* and *but* are also considered to be coordinating conjunctions. There is arguably in English, and proably in other languages as well, no absolutely clear-cut distinction between coordination and subordination, but a sliding of one into the other. For example, in the first sentence of this paragraph, *although* could be replaced by *but*, even though one is usually described as subordinating (*although*) and the other as coordinating (*but*).

The coordinating conjunction *and* is not simply 'additive' in meaning either; for example, the events in the two sentences joined by *and* may be temporally simultaneous or successive, eg

1. Harry is washing the dishes *and* Mary is ironing the clothes.
2. Harry made the coffee *and* Mary poured it out.

Both of these could be rephrased using a subordinating conjunction:

1a. *While* Harry is washing the dishes, Mary is ironing the clothes.
2a. *After* Harry had made the coffee, Mary poured it out.

According to the analysis proposed in Chapter 19, both the *while*-clause in 1a and the *after*-clause in 2a would be considered to be embedded sentences functioning as Adjunct. In 1 and 2, on the other hand, both sentences are regarded as independent, and so can be represented in a tree-diagram as:

If coordination slides in one direction into subordination, in the other it slides into independent, uncoordinated sentences. Example No 1 above could be written in either of the following ways:

1b. Harry is washing the dishes; Mary is ironing the clothes.
1c. Harry is washing the dishes. Mary is ironing the clothes.

In 1b the two sentences are 'coordinated' by the semi-colon; in 1c they are separate, uncoordinated sentences. In speech the distinction between 1b and 1c cannot be made. Separate sentences may also be linked by 'conjunctive adverbs', such as *moreover* or *additionally* in English for 'logical' addition, or *then* for temporal addition, eg

2b. Harry made the coffee. *Then* Mary poured it out.
2c. Harry usually makes the coffee. *Moreover* he does it very well.

Several possibilities thus exist for making 'additive' or 'coordinative' links between sentences, from mere juxtaposition to the use of a coordinating conjunction. It may be useful, therefore, to distinguish between coordination as a semantic relationship of an additive kind and coordination as a syntactic relation marked by conjunctions.

Sometimes the distinction between subordination and coordination is made according to the following criterion: in subordination some kind of grammatical change or marker must be present in the subordinate sentence, whereas in coordination no such marker is found in either sentence. In English, for example, some subordinate sentences have non-finite verb forms, or a modal verb (eg *should/would* in *if*-clauses), or a special tense in a sequence of tense rule (eg past perfect in *before/after*-clauses). In French, some subordinate sentences require the verb to be in the subjunctive mood, eg those introduced by the conjunctions *quoique* 'although', *pourvu que* 'provided that', *jusqu'à ce que* 'until'. Consider the following data (SIL 1980: F2) based on Engenni (Nigeria):

1. elegbeʃi bo nɛ ʃire   'The big cat ran'
   cat   big the ran
2. i   mɔni ga mi yia   na   'They saw me coming'
   they saw   I   came
3. mi yi   'I came'
       came
4. i demine gbe   ka mi zə   'They soon went home,
   soon   went-home   stayed   but I stayed'
5. owutumu wa   ga elegbeʃi demine raia   na 'The rat wants the cat to
   rat   wants   quickly go-away   go away quickly'
6. elegbeʃi bo nɛ wa ga ɔki dia na   'The big cat wants to eat'
                   he eats
7. elegbeʃi demine vai   'The cat soon went away'
8. elegbeʃi ika   ʃire ka owutumu gbɛri nɛ demine rai 'Those cats ran and the
           those   small   small rat quickly went
                                                            away'
9. amɔ anɔ mɔni   'This child saw it'
   child this

10. elegbeʃi bo ina le   yi ka owutumu nɛ mo   'These big cats came again
       these again   was-not   but the rat was not there'
11. amɔ gbɛri anɔ le wa   'This small child wants
                              some more'

12. elegbeʃi bo yi   'A big cat came'

In this data there are several examples which contain two sentences: Nos 2, 4, 5, 6, 8, 10. The remaining examples serve to elucidate those with two sentences. The latter are of two types: Nos 2, 5, 6 fall into one group, and Nos 4, 8, 10 into the other. The first group of examples involves subordination (or embedding) and the second coordination. In Nos 2, 5 and 6, besides the boundary markers of the embedded sentence—*ga* initially and *na* finally—there is also a suffix -*a* on the verb: the embedded sentence is thus both bounded and marked internally, which one might justifiably construe as evidence of subordination. In Nos 4, 8 and 10, on the other hand, the sentences are simply linked by *ka*, which is glossed as both *and* and *but* in English. We are, therefore, justified in regarding these examples as cases of coordinated sentences.

'Sentence' and 'clause'

Having discussed the coordination of sentences we can now make explicit the way in which we have used the terms 'sentence' and 'clause'. In some hierarchical (constituency) models of linguistic analysis (see Chapter 22), 'sentence' and 'clause' are regarded as separate levels of linguistic organisation, with 'sentence' as the higher level (larger unit) and 'clause' as the level below, so that sentences are composed of clauses and clauses are constituents of sentences. We have not used the terms in this way.

As we hinted in Chapter 13, when discussing relative clauses, we have used the term 'clause' only to refer to embedded or subordinate sentences (eg 'non-finite clause', 'adverbial clause', 'relative clause'). So, the term 'sentence' includes that of 'clause': clauses are sentences with a particular function that involves their embedding in other sentences or in phrases. Sentences, then, are any unit with the structure discussed in Chapters 10 and 11 (ie S P O, etc), and they may be independent or dependent, main or subordinate, non-embedded or embedded.

Ellipsis

One syntactic process that is often associated with coordination, though it is not exclusive to it, is ellipsis. In coordinated sentences, ellipsis involves the omission of an item from usually the second sentence that is a repetition of an item in the first sentence. For example, in "The workmen repaired the roof and mended the fences", the Subject (*the workmen*) has been omitted from the second sentence; in "Harry plays the violin and Mary the cello", the Predicator (*plays*) has been omitted. The items omitted from the second sentence are said to be 'recoverable' from the first. It is possible, though less common, at least in English, for ellipsis to occur in the first sentence of a coordinated pair; cf "Harry enjoys but Mary despises

'Coronation Street''', where the Object (*'Coronation Street'*) is omitted from the first sentence. In English it would appear that ellipsis may occur in the first sentence only with Objects. As stated, ellipsis is not confined to coordination; it is, for example, typical of conversational dialogue, eg A: "What is Harry doing?", B: "(Harry is) mowing the lawn".

Rules for ellipsis vary from lanaguage to language. It is not possible in English to omit just the perfect auxiliary (*have*) from a second sentence (*"Harry has painted the walls and Mary sewn the curtains"), whereas this is acceptable in German, eg "Hans hat die Wände angestrichen und Ulrike die Vorhänge genäht". Compare also: "Hans hat die Wände und Ulrike die Tür angestrichen' (*lit.* 'Hans has the walls and Ulrike the door painted')—'Hans has painted the walls and Ulrike the door'.

Phrase + phrase

Coordination is not confined to sentences; it is also found between phrases of the same type, eg between noun phrases or adjective phrases. Consider the following English examples:

1. one man and his dog.
2. a quite graceful and very powerful dancer.
3. the man in the white coat and the woman wearing the strange hat.
4. very carefully but not hesitantly.

Examples 1 and 3 comprise coordinated noun phrases. In No 1 the noun is in each case expanded by just one word (*man* by the numeral *one*, *dog* by the possessive identifier *his*). In No 3 both nouns are expanded by the definite article *the*, and the first noun is further expanded by a prepositional phrase (*in the white coat*), while the second noun is expanded by a present participle clause (*wearing . . .*). The second example is a noun phrase that includes coordinated adjective phrases (*quite graceful*, *very powerful*), both with adjectives expanded by an intensifying adverb. The fourth example is of coordinated adverb phrases, with the adverbs expanded by the intensifiers *very* and *not* respectively.

Not to be confused with the coordination of noun phrases is the 'apposition' of noun phrases, eg "my son, the pharmacist", where two noun phrases are juxtaposed but both have the same reference. In the case of the coordination of noun phrases, each noun phrase refers to a different entity, cf "my son and the pharmacist". Note the ambiguity of: "my son, the pharmacist and the undertaker", where the only clue to the triple coordination (ie three different people) is the lack of a comma after *pharmacist* (representing an alternative intonation patterning in speech).

Word + word

Words may also be coordinated within the same phrase. The words coordinated may be head words or words in the expansion of heads. Consider the following

English examples:

1. wet roads and pavements.
2. muddy and slippery roads.
3. over and under the fence.
4. very straight and fast.
5. this and that arrangement.

In the first example a noun phrase contains two nouns that are coordinated. The first noun is preceded by an adjective (*wet*), which may be taken to be expanding both nouns or just the first. In speech this can be made clear by the division of the utterance into tone-units: if it is spoken as one tone-unit the adjective refers to both nouns, if as two then only to the first and we have a case of coordinated noun phrases rather than of coordinated nouns. The second example is also a noun phrase; it contains coordinated adjectives, both expanding the noun *roads*. The adjectives are explicitly coordinated by *and*; they could be implicitly coordinated, without a conjunction, eg "muddy, slippery roads".

The third example is a prepositional phrase with coordinated prepositions. In this case the coordination must be explicit; a coordinating conjunction is obligatory, as it is in the remaining two examples. No 4 is either an adjective phrase or an adverb phrase (*straight* and *fast* belong to both word classes), with coordinated adjectives (adverbs), the first of which is preceded by *very*, which may be taken as expansion of both items or of just the first (cf No 1). The fifth example is a noun phrase in which the demonstrative identifiers are coordinated; they both expand the noun *arrangement*. Clearly there are restrictions on the words that may be coordinated; for example, articles are incompatibly coordinated (*"a and the arrangement"), though coordinated possessive identifiers would be possible ("my and your arrangements").

Finally, it should be noted that it is also possible to coordinate morphemes, though this possibility applies only to derivational morphemes, not to inflectional morphemes. For example, in English "under- and overcharged" the prefixes are coordinated, in German "das Ein- und Ausmarschieren" ('the marching in and out') similarly. Compare also: "pre- and postnatal", "de- and revaluation" in English. In German a similar coordination occurs with compound nouns, eg "Haus- und Gartenmöbel" ('house and garden furniture'), "Gemüse- und Blumengeschäft" ('vegetable and flower shop').

Exercise 41

Describe the relationships between sentences in the following data (SIL 1980: F3) based on Yakurr (Nigeria). Note: tone is marked in this data in the verb word only, ´ marks high tone, ` marks low tone.

1. odəm ɔ́kɔ̀ì   likol   'The man goes to the bush'
   man   he-goes bush
2. ókɔ́   epu   'He sees a monkey'
   he-sees monkey
3. epu éjí   kenjen   'The monkey eats a banana'
   he-eats banana

4. odəm ɔ́dɛ̀   wɛn   'The man calls a boy'
      he-calls boy

5. wɛn ótɔ̀   ekon   'The boy takes his gun'
      he-takes gun

6. nə ótà   ekon   'He will shoot (gun)'
      fut. he-shoot

7. ófì   epu   'He kills the monkey'
      he-kills

8. odəm ótɔ̀ epu   'The man takes the monkey'

9. yákɔ̀ì   ɛtɔ   'They go to the house'
      they-go house

10. wɛn òbə̀lì   epu   'The boy cuts up the monkey'
       he-cuts-up

11. odəm nə ɔ́nɔ̀n   ɛtɛn   'The man will cook the meat'
       he-cook meat

12. odəm nə ójí   ɛtɛn   'The man will eat the meat'
       he-eat

13. odəm ɔ́dɛ̀ wɛn ɛdɔ   wɛn ótɔ̀ ekon 'The man calls the boy and then the boy takes his
       and-then   gun'

14. odəm ótɔ̀ epu ɛdɔ yákɔ̀ì ɛtɔ   'The man takes the monkey and then they go to
       the house'

15. wɛn óbə̀lì epu ɛdɔ odəm nə ɔ́nɔ́n ɛtɛn 'The boy cuts up the monkey and then the man
       will cook the meat'

16. odəm ɔ́ɔkɔ̀ì   likol ókə̀ epu   'When the man goes to the bush he sees a
       when-he-goes   monkey'

17. óòkə̀ epu ɔ̀dɛ̀ wɛn   'When he sees a monkey he calls a boy'

18. wɛn óòtɔ̀ ekon ófì epu   'When the boy takes his gun he kills the monkey'

19. yáàkɔ̀ì ɛtɔ wɛn óbə̀lì epu   'When they go to the house the boy cuts up the
       monkey'

21. Function and form

In the remaining three chapters of this book we shall be reflecting on the way in which we do grammatical analysis and on the kinds of descriptive assumptions that underlie the analyses we have been making. The presupposition that will inform our discussions is that there is no one right way to do grammatical analysis and that the terms and categories used for making a grammatical description are chosen because they are judged to be representing the facts of the language as the analyst sees it. Another analyst may approach the same language data with a different set of terms and categories, a different linguistic perspective, a pair of linguistic spectacles of a different hue, and make an alternative description. Language is too complex a phenomenon, the human mind more capable and creative than we often think, to be put into the straightjacket of a single perspective, a single model of analysis and description. So, we will make explicit some of the analytical assumptions of this book and discuss some of the terms and categories employed in the descriptions. We begin, in this chapter, by looking at the distinction between 'function' and 'form'.

Sentences

The place in grammatical description where we have been most explicit about the distinction between 'function' and 'form' was in the analysis of sentences. We suggested that sentences could be regarded as being composed of a number of 'functional' places or slots, viz Subject, Predicator, Object, Complement and Adjunct (Chapter 11). We then said that these slots could be filled by certain categories or types of item. The Predicator slot is filled by a verb and any associated auxiliaries, aspectual or negative particles, and the like. The Subject and Object slots are filled by nouns or noun phrases, or by embedded sentences, or possibly by a pre/postpositional phrase. The Complement slot is filled by a noun (phrase) or by an adjective (phrase), or possibly by an embedded sentence. And the Adjunct slot is filled by an adverb (phrase), a pre/postpositional phrase, a noun (phrase) or an adverbial (embedded) sentence. We can summarise this in the following table:

Subject	:	noun, emb sent
Predicator	:	verb
Object	:	noun, pre/postp p, emb sent
Complement	:	noun, adjective, emb sent
Adjunct	:	adverb, pre/postp p, noun, emb sent

Alternatively, we can express the relationship in this way: a noun (phrase) is functioning as Subject in the sentence, an embedded sentence (eg non-finite clause) is functioning as Adjunct, etc. In other words, we regard the analysis of a sentence as comprising two parts: the identification of the elements that compose the sentence (noun (phrase), verb, embedded sentence, etc); and secondly, the function that each of those elements performs in the sentence (Subject, Complement, Adjunct, etc).

There are a number of reasons for making a dual analysis of this kind. First of all, there is no one-to-one correspondence between category (or form) and function; for example, a noun (phrase) may perform every sentence function apart from that of Predicator, embedded sentences of the same type may be found functioning as Subject, Object or Complement. Secondly, it is sometimes useful to be able to refer to an element performing a particular function, because this makes a more convenient descriptive statement; for example, it is easier to use the terms 'Subject' and 'Object' in talking about the formation of passive sentences than to have to devise a way of distinguishing the two noun phrases involved in the transformation of active to passive. The same is true for the description of sentence agreement, eg between Subject noun and verb functioning as Predicator.

The term 'function' is not to be equated with 'meaning', although labels such as 'Subject' or 'Object' betray some original semantic motivation. But these labels refer to syntactic functions. It may be argued, as indeed it has been by some linguists, that such labels are superfluous to a grammatical description of sentence structure; it is perfectly possible to make analyses and descriptions of sentences without invoking such functional terms. What we maintain is that a labelling with functional terms provides a useful additional descriptive perspective on sentence structure, that provides further insight into grammatical structuring and a useful set of labels when talking about certain grammatical processes or relationships, such as passivisation or agreement.

As for semantic labels applicable to sentence elements, we have used these from time to time in our analysis and description; for example, and perhaps more often than any of the others, the term 'Agent', referring to the instigator of an action. A further semantic label is that of 'Patient' or 'Undergoer', the participant affected by an action, or the participant that undergoes a process (eg "The doorkeeper (Agent) opened (action) the door (Patient)", "The apple (Patient) fell (process) from the tree (Source)"). These labels represent generalised semantic concepts and are sometimes referred to as 'logico-semantic' categories. They constitute a further perspective on the analysis of sentences, and they can be useful in certain kinds of discussion about grammatical phenomena; for example, it is useful to note that sentence elements retain their semantic identity under certain transformations while their syntactic-functional status may change, eg the Agent in a passive transformation.

Phrases

In our analysis of phrases we have not been nearly so consistent or explicit in distinguishing functional terms from formal (or category) terms, or in making a clear dual analysis. In fact, we have not consistently proposed 'phrase' as a level of analysis between sentence and word: we have used the term 'phrase' as a convenient shorthand label for a word and its expansion. In other words, we have proposed two fundamental levels of grammatical analysis: 'sentence' and 'word'.

We have treated words from two perspectives: their composition in terms of morphemes; and their combinability with each other in terms of classes. In undertaking the latter we have identified a number of classes (eg noun, adjective, adverb) whose members can function solely and directly as constituents in sentence structure, and a number of other classes (eg determiner, adjective, intensifying adverb) whose members serve to expand members of the first group of word classes.

It is these combinations of word + expansion that we have conveniently termed 'phrases'. 'Phrase' could be regarded as a level of grammatical organisation in a constituency model of grammar (see Chapter 22). And in that case, we could make a dual analysis, as for sentences. The word that undergoes expansion is often said to function as 'Head' of the phrase; so, in a noun phrase, the noun functions as Head; in an adjective phrase, the adjective functions as Head; and so on. The items that constitute the expansion (itself an informal functional label) are said to function as 'Attributive' or 'Modifier'. Sometimes, where it is relevant, a distinction is made between Modifier, occurring before the Head, and Qualifier, occurring after the Head, or between Pre-Modifier and Post-Modifier. For example, in the English noun phrase "three tense hours later", *hours* is functioning as Head, *three* and *tense* are functioning as Pre-Modifiers, and *later* is functioning as a Post-Modifier.

Most phrase types can be analysed into Head and Modifiers/Attributives, where the Head, occurring alone, is the minimal form of the phrase. Such a structure is said to be 'endocentric': one of the constituents may substitute minimally for the whole structure. There is another phrase type, however, which does not have this structure: the prepositional/postpositional phrase. We have suggested that this type of phrase has the analysis 'Prep/Postp + NP', where the NP is regarded as an embedded phrase in the pre/postpositional phrase. Note also that such a phrase is not 'endocentric' but 'exocentric' in structure, since both the Pre/Postposition and the NP are obligatorily present. Such phrases are said functionally to consist of Relator + Axis: the pre/postposition functions as Relator; the NP functions as Axis.

Since the functional differentiation at phrase level is not nearly as diverse as it is at sentence level, consisting fundamentally of two functional terms—Head and Attributive/Modifier, or Relator and Axis—it is arguable that the functional analysis of phrases is not so important. Certainly an analysis, displayed, say, in the form of a tree-diagram, could dispense with functional labels at phrase level and lose very little information. However, if 'phrase' is recognised as a level of grammatical organisation and a dual analysis in terms of function and form is proposed, then for the sake of consistency and completeness functional labels at phrase level are essential; and a greater degree of differentiation could be made, eg by distinguishing closed-class items (eg determiners) from open-class items (eg adjectives) in the premodification of noun phrases.

Words

Earlier we cited the analysis of words into morphemes as one of the two fundamental analyses that we have proposed in this book. And we should now ask whether the same dual analysis into function and form should be applied to the analysis of words. In a sense, our analysis of words has been a dual one. On the one hand, we have used terms like 'Root', 'Prefix' and 'Suffix' which could be regarded as functional labels; eg x-morpheme functions as Root in y-words. On the other hand, we have used terms like 'tense morpheme' or 'plural morpheme', to identify particular categories of morpheme. Strangely, though, these category labels have a distinctly semantic or functional ring to them.

The structure of words is parallel to that of phrases rather than to that of sentences. Words generally have an endocentric structure, so that a noun word, for example, will have a noun Root (ie noun functioning as Root) as the minimal and obligatory element, and the 'plural' morpheme will function as Prefix or Suffix. If a distinction needs to be made among Prefixes or Suffixes, when there is more than one in a word, then this is often done by referring to Prefix 1, Prefix 2, etc, numbering from the Root outwards, eg 'Prefix 2—Prefix 1—Root—Suffix 1—Suffix 2'.

A problem arises, though, in the analysis of words into morphemes, where the word is not analyseable into segments that correspond to the morphemes of which the word is said to be constituted. For example, the word form *is* in English is said to be '3rd person singular present tense' of *be*, but it is not possible to identify a segment that could be a Root or segments that could be Prefixes or Suffixes (presumably the latter, given the general structure of the verb word in English). In some words, then, it is possible only to identify what the structure is in terms of the morphemes that are present, not to specify a function for each morpheme, except perhaps for the Root (ie the Root of *is* is *be*).

Summarising, we can say that a syntactic unit may be subject to a dual analysis: in terms of the function of the elements in the unit; and in terms of the form or category of the elements. Take the following English example: "Our two children are feeding the ducks in the park down the road", the analysis of which we can display in a tree-diagram as follows:

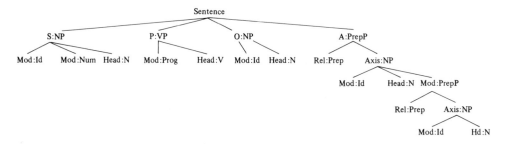

The labels on the left of the colon in each case are functional, those on the right categorial or formal.

22. Constituency and dependency

In this chapter we consider two general approaches to the analysis of grammatical structure that offer complementary perspectives on linguistic organisation. They are the 'constituency' approach and the 'dependency' approach. Most models of grammatical analysis adopt, implicitly or explicitly, a constituency approach, and it is this approach that has informed many of the analytical proposals in the present book. But, as I hope will become clear, dependency assumptions have also played their part. It is not my purpose to go into the history and development of these approaches to grammatical description, but rather to outline the assumptions underlying them and the insights they afford into the structure of language. We begin with constituency.

Constituency

The constituency approach to the analysis of grammatical structure begins from the assumption that grammatical units are related to each other syntactically in a relationship of composition. For example, sentences may be said to be composed of phrases; or alternatively, phrases are constituents of sentences. It is usual in such an approach to establish a hierarchy of units, sometimes called a 'rank scale' (ie a scale of ranks or levels); and the relationship of one rank to another is one of size and constituency. The rank scale often proposed for English, for example, has the following ranks:

Sentence	composed of one or more clauses
Clause	composed of one or more phrases
Phrase	composed of one or more words
Word	composed of one or more morphemes
Morpheme	

Reading downwards, the relationship between the units at one rank and those at the rank next below is one of constituency or composition. Reading upwards, the relationship between the units at one rank and those at the rank next above is one of function: morphemes function in words, words function in phrases, phrases function in clauses, clauses function in sentences. In this approach, a sentence can be exhaustively analysed at every level or rank. The phenomenon that we have called 'embedding' (Chapters 18 and 19), where a unit functions as the constituent of a unit at the same rank as itself or of a unit at a rank below itself, is termed 'rank-shifting' in this approach. The usual relationships of constituency operating between units at different ranks is superceded.

In its most mechanical form the constituency approach operates by means of a series of binary cuts on the basis of substitutability. For example, the English sentence "The big boys played football all afternoon" would be analysed as:

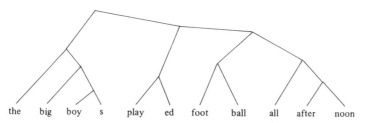

Such an analysis is unlabelled; indeed, it would be difficult to find terms with which to label many of the nodes in the tree. In this book we have operated with a more sophisticated constituency structure that pays full recognition to syntactic function (see Chapter 21) and grammatical labelling, and does not restrict analysis to binary cutting only.

We have operated a constituency approach in this book most consistently in the analysis of sentences, setting up functional slots (constituents) and specifying the categories of item that may fill them. We have also invoked a constituency approach in describing the structure of words in terms of their constituent morphemes, arranged in a particular order. Otherwise, in describing phrases for example, we have used a constituency approach where it seemed appropriate and useful in describing a particular syntactic relationship, eg in dealing with embedded units, where it is useful to say that a unit is composed of a word + an embedded unit as expansion, which in turn is composed of such and such units.

Clearly, constituency is an important relation in linguistic structure, and it is a perspective that accords with the facts of language. It is not a deception to say that a linguistic unit is composed of other linguistic units, that a relation of constituency holds between them: sentences are composed of words, if not of phrases; words are composed of morphemes, if not of morphs. We can speak of the constituents of a sentence or word, even if we cannot always specify unequivocally the order in which those constituents occur (eg variability in the order of sentence elements, one morph realising several morphemes). Structure can, then, be described in terms of constituency; but it is not the only way in which it can be approached.

Dependency

The dependency approach to the description of linguistic structure starts from the assumption that some elements determine the presence of other elements. Or to look at it the other way round, the presence of some elements is dependent on the presence of other elements. For example, an identifier (eg article, demonstrative identifier, possessive identifier) may not occur in English unless a noun is also present: the identifier is dependent on the noun. Dependency relations may be displayed by using a tree-style diagram, where the branches stand for the dependency relations, eg

noun
|
identifier

or by means of more horizontal, arrowed lines, where the direction of the arrow indicates the relationship of determination, eg

An assumption that is often made in a dependency approach to the analysis of sentences is that the Predicator/verb is the central element in the sentence, determining the presence of certain other elements, or on which other elements are dependent. For example, a ditransitive verb like *give* in English determines the presence of a Subject, a Direct Object and an Indirect Object; these are dependent on *give*. To take a concrete example: "Kirsten gave Nathan sweets" could be expressed in dependency terms as:

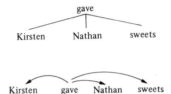

or as:

As we noted in Chapter 10, not all sentences contain verbs, eg No 9 from Exercise 22: "edei dori nɛ Ade" (lit. 'man tall the Ade'), ie 'The tall man is Ade'. Here, as so often with verbless sentences, we have an equative structure; and the two elements could be said to be mutually determining or dependent, ie

edei _____ dori nɛ   Ade

The other arrowed lines indicate that *dori* and *nɛ* are dependent on *edei*.

We have implied so far that determination and dependency are two sides of the same coin, complementary perspectives on the dependency relation. This is not exactly so, for while an element may be dependent on another element, it is not necessarily determined by it. For example, we could expand our earlier sentence in the following way: "Kirsten gave Nathan sweets yesterday in the park". While it is the case that *yesterday* and *in the park* are dependent on *gave*, they are not determined by it, since to omit these two elements does not render the sentence ungrammatical, as the omission of the Subject or either of the Objects would do. In discussing the determination and dependency of elements, then, a distinction is drawn between those elements that are obligatory, whose presence is determined (eg by the verb) and whose omission would render the structure ungrammatical, and those elements which are optional, whose presence is not determined and whose omission does not affect the grammaticality of the structure, but which are nevertheless dependent on some other element.

It is not always clear what is meant by 'determination'. Sometimes it is understood in a logico-semantic sense, rather as we used it in Chapter 10, eg *give* determines the presence of 'someone *give* something to someone', ie a giver, a thing given, and a person to whom it is given. Logically, we could extend this approach to include 'when given' and 'where given', and perhaps even 'how given' or 'why given', as elements that are determined by the verb *give*. Clearly this goes beyond the question of the grammaticality of any resulting structure (sentence), and perhaps becomes grammatically superfluous, since this kind of information may form part of almost any predication.

For this reason, 'determination' is often taken in a strictly syntactic sense, to refer to the elements required by another element for the resulting structure to be grammatical, ie to be acceptable as a complete and plausible structure by native speakers (though this definition of 'grammatical' begs a host of questions!). Thus the elements determined by *give* are the ones stated originally, ie the Subject and the two Objects. However, even this restriction on 'determination' is not without its difficulties. Consider a verb like *write* in English (cf Chapter 11): it would appear to be ditransitive like *give* ("Nathan is writing Kirsten a letter"), ie determining the presence of a Subject, an Indirect Object and a Direct Object. But either or both of the Objects may be omitted without rendering the sentence ungrammatical: "Nathan is writing a letter"/"Nathan is writing to Kirsten"/"Nathan is writing". In this case we can say either that *write* allows deletable Objects, or that the Objects are 'facultative' (an intermediate category between 'obligatory' and 'optional'), or that there are several verbs *write* in English, each determining a different set of elements.

Generally it appears to be the case that the elements determined by the verb in sentence structure are the Subjects, Objects and Complements; and the Adjuncts lie outside of the determination of the verb and are optionally occurring elements, though still dependent on it. This generalisation does not hold universally; for example, one of the uses of *put* in English determines the presence of an Adjunct of place ("We put the shoes outside the door"), the verb *last* determines the presence of an Adjunct of time ("The interview lasted two hours"). But these cases are in the minority, and our observation earlier that specification of time, place, manner, reason, etc may be made optionally for almost any predication generally holds.

Our discussion of dependency has centred on the analysis of sentences, and this is where the notion of dependency is most often invoked. But in principle a dependency analysis could be applied to any kind of linguistic structure. Indeed, our treatment of 'phrases' in terms of a word and its associated expansion implies dependency assumptions: a word determines or attracts other words into its orbit. So, "the old farm on the hill" could be analysed in a dependency approach as:

The preposition and noun are seen as mutually dependent, and so for prepositional phrases generally. The word "reintroductions" could be analysed as:

It will be noted that dependency trees have been written with the concrete lexical items, rather than with generalised grammatical labels, at the nodes. This reflects a tendency for the dependency approach to be concerned with actually occurring examples, at least as a first step to any generalisations, and to be an approach that fairly immediately is concerned about the operation of particular lexical items. However, there is in principle no difficulty in making generalised dependency statements, displayed in dependency trees, eg

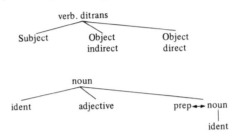

Complementary perspectives

A constituency analysis and a dependency analysis represent alternative, complementary perspectives on the grammatical structure of language. They are complementary in that neither approach exhaustively describes the structural facts of the grammar of a language. We have noted that relationships of constituency can be said to hold between syntactic units; equally, there are relationships of dependency between elements of syntax. Both are worthy of description. It is possible to make a description of the grammar of a language using either the constituency approach or the dependency approach, and the same grammatical 'facts' will be treated in both. But they will be treated in different ways, with different underlying assumptions, from different points of view: constituency and dependency are, thus, alternative perspectives on the analysis of language—complementary perspectives.

23. Indeterminacy and grammar

Rules, patterns and paradigms

In this book we have been concerned to reveal the scope of the topic of grammar, without making any particular claims to exhaustiveness or comprehensiveness. In doing this we have drawn on a number of languages by way of illustration, presenting the material as a set of data. On the basis of such data we have made statements to the effect that in such-and-such language this or that grammatical feature appears to exist, or this or that pattern or structure or process appears to be present. We have not presented anything like a comprehensive description of the grammar of any one language; if we had, we might have been more definite about some of our descriptive statements, and perhaps formulated our description, at least parts of it, in terms of grammatical 'rules'.

What do we mean by 'rule' in this context? We do not mean the kinds of prescription that we discussed in Chapter 1. By 'rule' we mean rather a descriptive statement that has general validity in the grammar. For example, we may formulate a rule of morphology in English which states that the 3rd person singular present tense form of verbs is marked by a suffix morpheme having the allomorphs /ɪz/, /z/, /s/ depending on phonological context. Or we may formulate a rule of syntax in English which states that possessive phrases marked by the clitic -s are placed in relation to the noun (possessed) in identical position to the possessive identifiers (*my*, *your*, etc).

Sometimes syntactic facts are described in terms of 'patterns' rather than of 'rules', as we did in Chapters 10 and 11 in discussing sentence types. Here the implication is that sentences (or whatever kind of syntactic structure) in a language are modelled according to one of the patterns. Sometimes the patterns are formulated in such a way as to indicate which elements are obligatory and which optional, either by marking obligatory elements with '+' and optional elements with '±', or by enclosing optional elements in brackets; eg 'NP: (identifier) (quantifier) (adjective) Noun (prep phrase)', or 'transitive sentence': +Subject +Predicator +Object ±Adjunct. Such statements of patterns could be reformulated in terms of rules, either discursively or in some kind of formula.

Similar to the notion of pattern is that of 'paradigm', associated in particular with morphology, where a list of morphological alternatives serves as a model or pattern for words belonging to the same class or subclass. For example, in Chapter 4 we presented a paradigm for the forms of the imperfect, present and future tenses of the verb *parler* 'speak' in French. This paradigm serves as a pattern for all so-called '-er' verbs in French. Such paradigms are often used in the description of highly inflecting languages like Latin or Greek, where a single suffix will often represent the realisation of several morphemes; eg the -o of Latin *amo* 'I love' is said to realise 1st person, singular number, present tense, indicative mood, active voice.

Indeterminacy

It is sometimes asserted that a language is a 'rule-governed system'. The implication of such a statement is that a language can be described exhaustively in terms of a set of rules, and that such a set of rules is closed. I would dispute both the assertion and its implications. Language is 'messy', it is characterised by indeterminacy. We have already noted (Chapter 1) that a language is not a homogeneous entity; but even having defined which variety of a language is being described, it still retains a fundamental indeterminacy. Indeed, this would be true even for the language of an individual speaker (sometimes called an 'idiolect'). Languages are indeterminate in a number of ways; we shall consider three of them: exceptions, context, and innovation.

Exceptions

Descriptive linguists are notorious for prefacing their descriptive statements with adverbs such as "normally", "usually" or "generally". These caveats are an implicit acknowledgement of the indeterminacy of language, and more particularly of the fact that grammatical statements frequently have exceptions, sometimes called 'irregularities'. To illustrate this point, let us take some of the grammatical 'rules' that we proposed earlier.

Our first 'rule' concerned the 3rd person singular present tense suffix on English verbs. There are two kinds of exception to the rule as we stated it. Firstly, there is a set of verbs that does not inflect in this way: the 'modal' auxiliary verbs, eg *may*, *can*, *must*. Indeed, a couple of verbs are variable in their inflection by this suffix: *need*, for example, tends to inflect in the positive ("She needs to go") but not in the negative ("She needn't go", but cf "She doesn't need to go"); and *dare* is even more variable, eg "He dares(to) go", "I don't think he dare/dares go", "He dares not go", "He daren't go". Secondly, the form of the suffix does not always follow the regular pattern, ie /ɪz/, /z/, /s/. Compare: *does* /dʌz/, which involves a vowel change /u→ʌ/ as well as the suffix; *has* /hæz/, which involves replacement of the final consonant /v→z/; *is* /ɪz/, which involves suppletion /bi→ɪz/. In each case it is a single lexical item that forms the 3rd person singular present tense in an irregular way.

Our second 'rule' concerned the placement of the possessive phrase in English. Consider the following noun phrase: "the bright cat's eyes". Here the identifier (*the*) and the adjective (*bright*) are attributives not to *cat* but to *eyes*; that is to say, *the bright cat's* is not a possessive phrase modifying *eyes*. One might say that the possessive phrase *cat's* has been placed exceptionally after an adjective instead of in its usual identifier position. However, one is more likely to argue in favour of regarding *cat's eyes* as a compound noun. A more difficult case is the following noun phrase attested by the author: "the high pilot's seat". Clearly, *the* and *high* expand *seat* rather than *pilot*. But an argument for *pilot's seat* as a compound could be more difficult to sustain than the one for *cat's eyes*.

Our third 'rule' concerned the formula for the pattern of transitive sentences in English. The formula indicates that Adjunct is optional in transitive sentences. But this is, to say the least, an ambiguous indication, since in a generalised formula of this kind optionality means either that Adjuncts may or may not be present in a transitive sentence depending on the free choice of the speaker, or that an Adjunct is (must be) present in some instances but not in others. In fact, the situation in English is more complex than those two alternatives imply. On the one hand, there are verbs where the Adjunct is obligatory, like *put* or *keep* (eg "She put the key *into the lock*", "They keep the key *under the mat*"). On the other hand, with the great majority of transitive verbs, Adjuncts are entirely optional, subject to contextual constraints. But intermediate between these two poles, there are a number of verbs, especially concerned with movement or propulsion, where the Adjunct is more-or-less obligatory, eg *kick*, *throw*, *drive* (eg "He threw the ball (over the fence)"). Such gradations are difficult to capture in terms of rules.

Finally, we presented a paradigm for the '-er' verbs in French. The assumption of such a paradigm is that all verbs forming their infinitives in the *-er* suffix show the same forms in the specified tenses as the paradigm verb. One does not have to look far to find exceptions to such paradigms; for example, the verb *aller* 'go', which forms its present tense as follows: je vais, tu vas, il/elle va, nous allons, vous allez, ils/elles vont. Only the 1st and 2nd person plural forms correspond to the paradigm. *Aller* conforms to the paradigm in the imperfect tense (j'allais, etc), but changes the stem in the future tense: j'irai, tu iras, etc.

Context

Descriptions of the grammar of a language tend to be made on the basis of individual sentences devoid of context. Grammar writers usually regard their task as the description of 'sentence grammar', and regard this as justification for dealing with isolated sentences. However, if context is taken into account many of the formulations of sentence grammars need to be modified in various ways. In discussing coordination (Chapter 20) we noted the process of ellipsis, which can lead to the omission of normally obligatory items under the conditions of coordination. And we noted also that ellipsis is not confined to coordination, but may occur across as well as within sentence boundaries, especially in spoken discourse.

In Chapter 22 we discussed the case of the verb *write* in English, which appears to be used intransitively, transitively and ditransitively. We suggested that one solution might be to consider that there are three verbs *write* in English, depending on which sentence pattern *write* enters. But if we note that the context of the sentence with the verb *write* will afford an explanation of this indeterminacy in the elements occurring with it, then we can describe the syntactic operation of *write* in terms either of what normally happens, with attendant variations, or of certain tendencies, depending on context.

There are many other instances where context will reveal an instability in a grammatical 'rule'. For example, *give* is normally a ditransitive verb, but someone passing a collecting box for a charity might remark to a companion, "Have you given yet?" (where *give* is intransitive (?)), and might receive the reply, "I never give to charity" (where *give* has a Subject and an Indirect (?) Object). Or consider *put*, which we noted earlier normally requires an obligatory Adjunct. In an appropriate context, however (parent to child, perhaps), one might say, "Don't throw it, put it" (where the Adjunct is absent).

If, as descriptive linguists, we are to take what language users actually speak and write as the data on which we base our descriptions, then we cannot avoid taking context into account, not necessarily incorporating it into our descriptions, but being aware both that the data itself may be skewed by its context and that the rules we formulate may be unstable and indeterminate within some linguistic or situational context.

Innovation

The grammar, or indeed other parts, of a language may be indeterminate because it is undergoing change initiated by innovation. No living language (ie one used in the ordinary affairs of everyday life) exists in a steady state. We have already noted that a language comprises a number of varieties, and these varieties inevitably interact; similarly, a language may exist in a contact situation, with bilingual speakers, and interaction is again highly likely if not inevitable. So, at any point in time, the grammar of a (variety of a) language will contain features and structures that will be used by some of the speakers but not by others.

Consider the verb *promise* in English. For some native speakers of English *promise* may enter a ditransitive sentence pattern, eg "She promised him to phone that evening" (S P Oi Od). But for other native speakers such a sentence is unacceptable; and it is indeed syntactically odd in English. All other verbs that enter this pattern with an infinitive clause functioning as Direct Object (eg "She *asked* him to phone that evening", "She *told* him to phone that evening") have the Indirect Object as the implied Subject of the infinitive clause. With *promise* the implied Subject of the infinitive clause is the same as the Subject of *promise* itself. A descriptive linguist has to recognise an indeterminacy here in the grammar of English, arising out of the disputed acceptability of *promise* in ditransitive sentence patterns.

Another example of disputed usage in the standard variety of English is found in the preposition that is used after the adjective *different*. Traditionally, and prescriptively, *different* has been followed by the preposition *from*. But this preposition vies with *to* and *than* in the usage of native speakers. Similarly, a traditional distinction is made between the comparative quantifiers *less* and *fewer*, with *less* combining with mass nouns (eg "less cheese", "less milk") and *fewer* combining with countable nouns (eg "fewer people", "fewer trains"). This distinction is now being undermined because educated native speakers, including those in the public media, are using *less* in both contexts (ie "less people", "less trains").

It is often easier to recognise changes brought about by innovation in retrospect, than to detect such innovations in the present. We can, for example, trace the changes in the personal pronoun system of English that led to the loss of the singular/plural, informal/formal distinction in the 2nd person pronouns, the replacement of *thou/thee*, *ye/you* by the single *you* form. One wonders how the pronoun system will emerge from current concerns to eradicate 'sexist bias' from English, which manifests itself in the written form *s/he* (meaning 'she or he') or in the use in some contexts of the 3rd person plural pronoun to refer to a single person of either sex, eg "If anyone comes ask *them* to wait", "A member shall be deemed to have resigned if *they* fail to pay the subscription within three months of the due date".

Readers may have noticed that I have opted in this book to use *data* as a (singular) mass noun, rather than as the alternative plural countable noun ("these data", etc).

Envoi

This chapter has emphasised the instability and indeterminacy of grammar. It has not thereby meant to imply that one cannot talk in terms of grammatical 'rules'. But it has meant to maintain that the grammar of a (variety of a) language is not a stable, steady-state system. The grammar of any language is fuzzy. That is in the nature of language, and it is a reflection of the fact that the human mind is able to cope with considerable messiness and indeterminacy in the systems with which it operates. I would go further and say that it is a reflection of the fundamental 'creativity' of the human mind, itself a reflection of the fact that human beings are created "in the image of God". Bringing theology and linguistics together, the study of language is an investigation of the creative handiwork of God in his endowments of humankind.

Further reading

The hints on further reading are kept deliberately brief. The choice appeared to be between giving a vast list to illustrate the variety of work that has been undertaken on grammar of both a theoretical and descriptive kind, and leading the reader on to the next stage in his or her investigation of grammar. It was decided to do the latter. The list is divided into three.

1. Analysis

A book with a similar aim to the present one, but at a more advanced level is:

K L Pike & E G Pike, *Grammatical Analysis*, Summer Institute of Linguistics, 1977.

2. General discussions

Three books are recommended under this section:

D J Allerton, *Essentials of Grammatical Theory*, Routledge & Kegan Paul, 1979.
P H Matthews, *Morphology*, 1974.
P H Matthews, *Syntax*, 1981.

These last two are published in the 'Cambridge Textbooks in Linguistics' series by Cambridge University Press.

The bibliographies in all these books will give the reader an indication of the variety of the work undertaken in grammar.

3. Grammars

Grammatical descriptions of the well-known European languages are readily available, although some are more informed by trends in modern linguistic description than others, eg

R Quirk, S Greenbaum, G Leech, J Svartvik, *A Grammar of Contemporary English*, Longman, 1972.

For descriptions of less well-known languages, the reader is advised to consult the volumes published in the 'Lingua Descriptive Linguistics Series' by the North Holland Publishing Company, Amsterdam, the first of which was by D C Derbyshire on *Hixkaryana*, in 1979.

Many descriptions of minority languages are published by the Summer Institute of Linguistics itself, and a catalogue is available from the SIL Bookstore: 7500 West Camp, Wisdom Road, Dallas, Texas 75236, USA.

Key to exercises

Exercise 1

1. acceptable.
2. unacceptable: adjectives *big* and *small* should precede nouns *dog* and *puppy* respectively.
3. unacceptable: *not* should precede *eats*, and should itself be preceded by *does*, causing *eats* to become *eat*.
4. acceptable, grammatically, although nonsense semantically.
5. unacceptable: adverb *beautifully* cannot go with a noun; *receiving* as a verb either needs *is* before it, or should have the form *receives*; preposition *into* does not go with a noun after quantifier (*many*).
6. acceptable.

Exercise 2

state, statement, restate, restatement, stately, stateliness.
large, enlarge, enlargement, reenlarge, reenlargement, largely.
treat, treatment, retreatment, entreat.

Exercise 3

Big, *fast* and *tall* belong together, because they can have the endings *-er* and *-est*, meaning 'more' and 'most'.

Read, *sell* and *grow* belong together, because they can have the endings *-s* and *-er* meaning 'he/she/it does' and 'person who does'.

Exercise 4

Taburete 'chair' and *pan* 'bread' belong together, because they can take the initial constituent ʃ- along with the endings *-be* and *-du*, to mean 'his' or 'our'.

-kaa- and *-ʒoonē-* belong together, because they must have one of the initial constituents *ru-*, *zu-*, *bi-*, *ku-* along with one of the endings *-du* or *-be*, to indicate tense (initial) and person (final).

Exercise 5

There are three word classes:

1. Verb, functioning as head of the Predicator (the first element in the clause), and including *kukrē* 'eats', *ape* 'works'.
2. Noun, functioning as head of the Subject (the second element in the clause), and including *kokoi* 'monkey', *kra* 'child', *mɨ* 'man'.
3. Attribute, functioning as attributive in both Predicator and Subject, and including *ratʃ* 'big'/'a lot', *mɛtʃ* 'good'/'well', *punui* 'bad'/'badly', *piŋetʃ* 'old'/'a long time'.

Exercise 6

There are three genders, marked by an ending on the numeral:

1. marked by -*kʔe* includes *hun* 'paper', *jopo* 'leaf', *wah* 'tortilla'.
2. marked by -*tu* includes *tsitam* 'pig', *winik* 'man', *mut* 'bird'.
3. marked by -*tsʔit* includes *hin* 'alligator', *tsan* 'snake'.

Gender 1 appears to contain nouns referring to flat objects, Gender 2 to animates apart from reptiles, and Gender 3 to reptiles.

Exercise 7

		Noun	Dem	*-mbini*
Gender 1	sing	u-	u-	
-*bɔti* 'chief'				
-*ni* 'person'	pl	bi- -ib	bi-	
Gender 2	sing	di-	di-	
-*yin* 'name'				
-*bil* 'seed'	pl	a-	ŋi-	
Gender 3	sing	ku- -u	ku-	
-*saa*- 'farm'				
-*kabu*- 'basket'	pl	ti- -ti	ti-	

Exercise 8

Verbs: -*sem* 'speak', -*on* 'see'.
Person Prefixes: *ni*- '1st person singular', *wu*- '2nd person', *a*- '3rd person singular', *wa*- '3rd person plural'.
Tense Prefixes: *na*- 'present', *li*- 'past', *taka*- 'future'.

Note the order of constituents: Subject person—Tense—Object person—Verb
'they saw him' = "waliaon".

Exercise 9

Verbs: *chaya*- 'arrive', *puñu*- 'sleep'.
Person Suffix: -*ni* '1st person singular', -*ngui* '2nd person'.
Tense Suffix: -*rca* 'past', ('present' unmarked).
Aspect Suffix: -*cu* 'continuous', *mi*- 'definitive', -*mu* 'locative', -*char* 'dubitative'.

Order of constituents: Verb—locative—continuous—past—person—definitive/dubitative.

Exercise 10

Bound pronouns: *u*- Subject pronoun, always occurs.
yi- Object pronoun, occurs if no free object pronoun, or with free object pronoun for emphasis.
Free pronouns: *yena* Subject pronoun, emphatic.
yona Object pronoun, if with *yi*- then emphatic.

Exercise 11

Nouns: *diaga* 'ear', *ñee* 'foot', *ʒigi* 'chin', *ʒike* 'shoulder'.
Possessives: *-be* '3rd person singular masculine', *-du* '1st person plural', *-luʔ* '2nd person singular', *-tu* '2nd person plural'.
Number: *ka-* 'plural'.

Order of morphemes: Plural Affix—Root—Possessive Affix.

Exercise 12

Verb Root: *-da* 'give', *-siʔju* 'cut'.
Tense Affix: *ku-* 'future', *n-* 'present', *ngu-* 'past'.
Aspect Affix: *-j-* 'cause' (infix occurring after initial consonant of verb root).
Person Affix: ~ '1st person singular' (suprafix of nasalisation, occurring on final vowel of root), *-ba* '1st person plural exclusive', *-ō* '1st person plural inclusive', *-wō* '2nd person plural', '2nd/3rd person singular' unmarked.

Exercise 13

The first element (root) in the compound loses its initial vowel. The initial vowel of the second element is transferred to the beginning of the compound; eg *eci* + *ɛraŋa* → *ɛcíraŋa*.

If the first element ends in a consonant (Nos 2 and 3), this is deleted on compounding; eg *ɔbɔːk* + *ɛdɔŋɔ* → *ɛbɔːdɔŋɔ*.

Exercise 14

There are three derivational suffixes, attached to the verb root:

-dwu 'instrument' (ie the thing with which the action is performed).
-gwu 'locative' (ie the place where the action is performed).
-swu 'agent' (ie the person who performs the action).

All the suffixes derive nouns from the verb root.

One might, perhaps, regard *-wu* as a general 'nominaliser' suffix, with *-d*, *-g*, *-s* realising the specific meanings of 'instrument', 'locative' and 'agent'.

Exercise 15

Verb Roots: *-ita* 'see', *-maka* 'give'.
Person Prefix: *ni-* '1st person singular subject', *netʃ-* '1st person singular object', *ti-* '2nd person singular subject', *mits-* '2nd person singular object', *nan-* '2nd person plural subject', *k-* '3rd person singular masculine object' (Note: '3rd singular neuter object' is unmarked).
Honorific Affixes: *on-* '1st level—Sir', *-tsikah* '2nd level with *on*——honoured Sir', *-tihtsinoh* '3rd level with *on*——most honoured Sir'.

All affixes are inflectional.
Order of morphemes:

> Subject Person—Object Person—1st level—Verb Root—2nd/3rd level
> Honorific   Honorifics

Exercise 16

The allomorphs of the 'past tense' morpheme are as follows for each verb:

1. /d/ 2. /īd/ 3. /t/ 4. /d/ 5. /īd/ 6. /t/ 7. /d/ 8. /ī→eī/ 9. /æ→ɔ, tʃ→t/ 10. /ø/ 'zero'.

There are three variants of the suffix: /t/, /d/, /īd/.

Nos 8 and 9 involve replacement of sounds, the root vowel and in No 9 additionally the final consonant. In No 10, the allomorph is said to be 'zero', ie there is no overt mark of the 'past tense'.

Exercise 17

The 'plural' morpheme has two allomorphs: /lar/, which occurs after a previous /u, ɨ, a, o/ vowel (ie a mid back vowel); and /ler/, which occurs after a previous /i, y, e, ø/ vowel (ie a front vowel):

$$\{\text{plural}\} \to \frac{/\text{ler}/ \text{ after front vowels}}{/\text{lar}/ \text{ elsewhere}}$$

The '2nd person possessive' morpheme has four allomorphs: /un/, which occurs after /u, o/ (ie back rounded vowels); /ɨn/, which occurs after /ɨ, a/ (ie mid back unrounded vowels); /yn/, which occurs after /y, ø/ (ie front rounded vowels); /in/, which occurs after /i, e/ (ie front unrounded vowels):

$$\left\{\begin{array}{l}\text{2nd person}\\ \text{possessive}\end{array}\right\} \to \begin{array}{ll} /\text{yn}/ & \text{after front rounded vowels}\\ /\text{in}/ & \text{after front unrounded vowels}\\ /\text{un}/ & \text{after back rounded vowels}\\ /\text{ɨn}/ & \text{elsewhere}\end{array}$$

These morpheme variants illustrate a general feature of 'vowel harmony' in Turkish: within a particular word, the vowels tend to be all of the same general type.

Exercise 18

Verb Roots: *-bani-* 'wake up', *-dʒela-* 'find', *-kaa-* 'write', *-ree-* 'go out', *-yubi-* 'look for', *-ʒooñe-* 'run'.
Person Suffix: *-be* '3rd person singular masculine', *-du* '1st person plural'.
Tense Prefix: *bi-* 'past', *ka-/ku-* 'present continuous', *ri-/ru-* 'present', *za-/zu-* 'future'.

{present continuous} → /ka/ occurs with the following verb stems: *-bani-* 'wake up', *-dʒela-* 'find', *-ree-* 'go out'
/ku/ occurs elsewhere.

{present} → /ri/ occurs with the same verb stems as /ka/ 'present continuous'
/ru/ occurs elsewhere.

{future} → /za/ occurs with the same verb stems as /ka/ 'present continuous'
/zu/ occurs elsewhere.

Exercise 19

$$\left\{\begin{array}{l}\text{3rd person singular}\\ \text{masculine possessive}\end{array}\right\} \to \begin{array}{ll} /\text{hi}/ & \text{before stem-initial /ʔ/ (Nos 7, 8, 17).}\\ /\text{ij}/ & \text{before a stem-initial non-nasal vowel (Nos 4,}\\ & \text{5, 10, 16).}\\ /\text{iñ}/ & \text{before a stem-initial nasalised vowel (Nos 1,}\\ & \text{6, 9, 14, 15).}\\ /\text{i}/ & \text{elsewhere (ie before a stem-initial consonant).}\end{array}$$

All these allomorphs are phonologically conditioned.

$$\left\{\begin{array}{c}\text{3rd person singular}\\ \text{masculine reflexive}\\ \text{possessive}\end{array}\right\} \rightarrow$$

/ŋw/	occurs with the following noun stems: *āta* 'home', *ēmbiʔu* 'food'.
/gw/	occurs with the following noun stems: *ape* 'track', *upa* 'lying place', *iviri* 'younger brother', *ʔaŋgwe* 'shadow'.
/o/	elsewhere (Nos 1–11).

These allomorphs are morphologically conditioned.

Exercise 20

nak 'without' and *teen* 'with' could be considered particles.
-t 'to', *-dei* 'to(wards)', *-gaa* 'for' could be considered clitics.

Exercise 21

1. *someone* write *something* to *someone* OR *someone* write *someone something*.
   The thing written and/or the person written to may be omitted; eg "Jim is writing (a letter) (to his girlfriend)".
2. *someone* win *something* OR *someone* win *something* from *someone*.
   Eg "Jim has won the race", "Jim won the marbles from John". In the case of the first pattern, the something may be omitted according to context.
3. *someone* spend *some amount* on *something/someone*.
   Eg "Jim has spent £30 on shirts/on his girlfriend". The thing/person on which an amount is spent may be omitted.
4. *someone* wait *some amount of time* for *someone/something*.
   Eg "We have been waiting thirty minutes for you/the bus". The person/thing being waited for or alternatively the amount of time may be omitted.
5. *someone* invite *someone* to *something*.
   Eg "We have invited our colleagues to lunch". The 'to something' may be replaced by *somewhere*, eg "They invited him into the living room", or by *to do something*, eg "They invited him to give a speech".
6. *someone* clean *something*.
   Eg "The workman cleaned the machine".
7. *someone* fight (against) *someone/something*.
   Eg "The French fought (against) the Prussians/social injustice". Both participants may be combined in a single plural or co-ordinated noun (phrase), eg "They/The French and the Prussians are fighting".
8. *someone* report *something* to *someone*.
   Eg "The shopkeeper reported the robbery to the police". A slightly different meaning of 'report' is implied in: *someone* report to *someone*, eg "You just report to the supervisor".

Exercise 22

1. Equative.
2. Intransitive or possibly Locative (adverbial of 'place' after verb).
3. Stative/Descriptive (here the sentence has only noun + verb, but the verb is a 'descriptive' verb).
4. Transitive (the adverbial of 'place' adds gratuitous information).
5. Transitive.
6. Stative/Descriptive (like No 3).
7. Intransitive or Locative (like No 2).
8. Intransitive.
9. Equative (cf No 1).

Exercise 23

1. Intransitive (but with an adverbial of 'direction', cf No 8).
2. Transitive.
3. Equative (note verbless).
4. Transitive.
5. Locative (verbless, with adverbial of 'place').
6. Locative (like No 5).
7. Equative (like No 3).
8. Intransitive (like No 1).
9. Locative (like No 5).
10. Transitive (like No 4, but with gratuitous adverbial of 'place').

Exercise 24

1. The shipyard (S) is building (P) a new oil-tanker (O)—transitive.
2. Harry (S) is sitting (P) in the garden (A)—locative.
3. The children (S) will put (P) their muddy boots (O) on the kitchen floor (A)—transitive/locative.
4. Susan (S) is (P) a first-class journalist (C)—stative.
5. Last night's storm (S) blew over (P) the tree in the corner (O)—transitive.
6. The committee (S) has appointed (P) Edward (O) as its secretary (C)—transitive/stative.
7. Our parking time (S) expired (P) five minutes ago (A)—temporal.
8. Harry (S) was telling (P) us (O) a funny story (O)—ditransitive.
9. The branch (S) is breaking (P)—intransitive.
10. My coat (S) is (P) the brown one (C)—equative.

Exercise 25

1. xóots (O:NP) saxwaa.áx (P:VP) dzeeyáak (Optional A: Adverb)—transitive.
2. Juneau-dé (A:Noun) kukgwaatèen (P:VP)—intransitive or locative.
3. kúnax (Optional A:Adverb) kusi.áat' (P:VP)—impersonal or stative.
4. tlax (Optional A:Adverb) a (S:Pronoun) yáanax ee (A:NP) wdixwétl (P:VP)—descriptive or stative.
5. ee xòonee (C:NP)—equative.
6. aatlèin dáana (S:NP) doo jèewoo (A:NP)—locative or possessive.

Exercise 26

NP: noun—numeral—quantifier—demonstrative.

Exercise 27

NP: demonstrative—numeral—adjective—noun.
Not more than two modifiers co-occur.
The minimal noun phrase is the noun alone.

Exercise 28

The possessor phrase precedes the noun being possessed (although the numeral postmodifies the noun, eg Nos 5 and 8). However, it is not the possessor phrase that is marked, but the noun being possessed. It is marked by the transfer of the (gender/classifier) prefix on the noun to become a suffix on the same noun, eg *ubɔti* (No 1) → *bɔtiu* (No 2), *kukuntuu* (No 12) → *kuntuuku* (No 13). In the case of *kusaau*, however, the final *-u* disappears when the *ku* is suffixed (cf Nos 8 and 9). Note that there is no possessive identifier (like English *his*), but that possessor pronouns act just like nouns (Nos 13 and 14: *u* presumably = 'he'). Note also that possession can recur, with the same rules operating (Nos 14 and 15).

Exercise 29

Possessive phrase: it is positioned after the noun (plus any modifiers) that is being possessed; the phrase is marked by a *g-* prefix on the head noun, eg *ewo ɛpa gɔi* 'the child's two dogs'; recursion may occur, eg *gada gɔlɛ* 'of the father of the compound'.

Relative clause: it is positioned after the noun (plus any modifiers) to which it refers; it is introduced by the particle *ni* (functioning as 'relative pronoun'), which replaces the modified noun in the relative clause; only examples occur in which the modified noun is implied Subject in the relative clause.

Exercise 30

This data illustrates expansion of adjectives by means of phrases and clauses. Phrases are positioned before the adjective they expand. The phrase may be a noun phrase in either the accusative case (No 5), the genitive case (No 2), or the dative case (No 1). The phrase may be a prepositional phrase, with the noun phrase in the case appropriate to the preposition, eg *zu* + dat (No 3), *gegen* + acc (No 4), *von* + dat (No 7), *auf* + acc (No 8), *für* + acc (No 9). The clauses—infinitive and *dass* clauses—are positioned after the adjective, but the position before the adjective is taken by a clause-correlative, *es* if the adjective is not associated with a preposition (No 6) or *da*-preposition if the adjective is associated with a preposition (No 10).

Exercise 31

Locatives and temporals are expressed by means of adverbs and prepositional phrases.

Locative adverbs: *ká* 'there', *kɨn* 'here'.
Temporal adverbs: *kà* 'then', *maŋ* 'again', *ufofo* 'yesterday'.
Prepositional phrases are formed with a preposition (eg *yè* 'from', 'since'; *k'* 'to') followed either by a noun (eg *k' utyen* 'to the farm') or by an adverb (eg *yè kɨn* 'from here', *yè ufofo* 'since yesterday').

Exercise 32

1. Participle clause (No 4) expressing temporal relation.
2. Temporal point-of-time clause introduced by *kun* 'when', with verb in past perfect tense (No 5).
3. Conditional clause introduced by *jos* 'if', with verb in present/future tense; and verb in main clause in present tense (No 7).
4. Purpose clause with infinitive verb form (No 9).

Exercise 33

There is agreement in the noun phrase with respect to gender and number, marked by suffixes as follows:

		Dem	Noun	Adj
Gender 1: masc				
menino 'boy'	sing	-e	-o	-o
vestido 'dress'	pl	-es	-os	-os
Gender 2: fem				
menina 'girl'	sing	-a	-a	-a
galinha 'hen'	pl	-as	-as	-as

A further generalisation could be made for the agreement in the plural, viz that in both genders for all elements the plural number agreement is marked by the addition of the *-s* suffix.

Exercise 34

There is agreement in the sentence between Subject and Predicator, with respect to gender and number, and marked by prefixes in the Subject noun and the verb as follows:

		Noun	Verb	
Gender 1				
-ñi 'elephant'	sing	o-	o-	(Nos 1, 2)
-jinɔŋ 'man'	pl	a-	ma	(Nos 4, 10)
Gender 2				
-ten 'animal'	sing	e-	e-	(No 3)
	pl	n-	i-	(No 8)

There is agreement in the noun phrase between noun, demonstrative and numeral, with respect to gender and number, marked by prefixes as follows:

		Noun	Dem	Num	
Gender 1	sing	o-	ŋw-		(No 5)
	pl	a-	mb-	a-	(No 6)
Gender 2	sing	e-	nd-		(No 4)
	pl	n-	nj-	n-	(No 8)

Exercise 35

Interrogative mood (polar questions) is signalled by the clitic *-o* attached to the final word in the sentence (Nos 2, 4, 6, 8).

Exercise 36

Passive sentences have a special form of the verb phrase: *be* + past participle. The Agent of the action is placed finally in a prepositional phrase introduced by *by* (Nos 1, 2, etc). The Agent may be omitted (Nos 4, 5, 7, 8), either because it is being suppressed or because it is unknown.

Ditransitive sentences may have either of the Objects (Direct or Indirect) made Subject of a passive transform (No 2—Indirect Object, No 3—Direct Object).

Noun phrases in Adjunct prepositional phrases may be made Subjects of passive sentences (Nos 6, 7), thus being exceptions to the rule that only transitive sentences may be passivised.

Exercise 37

The structure of the NP is:

adjective—NOUN—numeral—possessive phrase.

The possessive phrase, a prepositional phrase introduced by the preposition 'da' 'of', is embedded in the NP.

Exercise 38

Embedding occurs in: (1) postpositional phrase, eg "tɔhɔn zen ni" ('in the large village'), where the noun phrase *tɔhɔn zen* is embedded in the postpositional phrase; (2) the noun phrase, eg "koor zen dam zen" ('the tall chief's large house'), where the possessive phrase *koor zen* is embedded as part of the expansion of the noun *dam*—the possessive phrase appears to be marked merely by its position, before the noun being expanded, with other expansion (*viz* adjective) coming after the noun.

Exercise 39

This data contains embedded sentences as Object (Nos 5, 6, 8, 10). They are marked by the regular Object marker *-ra* suffixed to the verb word (order of sentence elements is OV). Otherwise the embedded sentence bears no other marker, except its appropriate position in the sentence in which it is embedded.

Exercise 40

This data contains embedded sentences functioning as Adjunct. The embedded sentences are in the form of what might be termed 'participle clauses'. No conjunctions are used (although they feature in the English glosses). The verb in the embedded sentence takes a special suffix: *-spa* if the Subject of the embedded sentence is the same as the Subject of the main sentence (Nos 1, 3, 5, 7); *-jpi* if the Subject of the two sentences is different (Nos 2, 4, 6, 8). The embedded sentence as Adjunct appears to take up initial position in the main sentence. The circumstantial meaning of the embedded sentence is deducible from: (1) the tense/aspect of the verb in the main sentence; (2) the aspect of the verb in the embedded sentence, eg the use of *-cu*, the continuous aspect suffix, in Nos 7, 8 (cf the verb of the main sentence in No 3).

Exercise 41

There are both embedded sentences and coordinated sentences in this data. Coordinated sentences are joined by the conjunction ɛdɔ 'and then'; there is no difference between a sentence when it is coordinated and when it is not (Nos 13–15).

Embedded sentences in this data are adverbial clauses functioning as Adjuncts of time in the independent/main sentences (Nos 16–19). These embedded sentences are marked as such in the verb word: the vowel of the first syllable of the verb word is doubled and bears a High + Low tone instead of a High tone; additionally, a High tone on the second syllable of the verb word is changed to a Low tone. Compare: ókɔ́ 'he sees' (No 2) with óòkɔ̀ 'when he sees' (No 17); yákɔ̀ì 'they go' (No 9) with yáàkɔ̀ì 'when they go' (No 19).

Phonetic symbols

The symbols included in this list are those used in data and examples, which do not feature in the Roman alphabet.

Consonants

ʈɖ	retroflex plosives
ʔ	glottal stop
ᵽ,ƀ/β	bilabial fricatives
θð	dental fricatives (as in English '*th*in', '*th*en')
ʃʒ	palato-alveolar fricatives (as in English '*sh*ip', 'plea*s*ure')
ɳ	retroflex nasal
ñ	palatal nasal
ŋ	velar nasal (as in English 'si*ng*')
ɭ	retroflex lateral
ɫ	velarised lateral (as in English 'pu*ll*')
ɽ	retroflex 'r'

Vowels

ɪ	close front spread vowel (as in English 'b*i*t')
ø	half-close front rounded vowel (as in French 'p*eu*', German 'sch*ö*n')
ɛ	half-open front spread vowel (as in French 'l*ai*t')
ɨ	close central spread vowel
ə	mid central spread vowel (as in English '*a*head')
ʊ	close back-rounded vowel (as in English 'b*oo*k')
ɔ	half-open back rounded vowel (cf English 'l*aw*')
ʌ	half-open back spread vowel (cf English 'b*u*t')

Diacritics

˜	nasalisation
¨	umlaut
ç	cedilla
ˏ	palatalisation (eg ţ)
´	acute accent or high tone
`	grave accent or low tone

Indexes

GENERAL INDEX

141

INDEX OF LANGUAGES